more natural michigan

A nature-lover's guide to 141 wildlife sanctuaries, arboretums, nature preserves, wilderness areas, recreation areas, gardens, parks, and other natural attractions.

by
tom powers

Friede Publications

More Natural Michigan

Copyright, 1992, by Tom Powers and Barb Powers

Friede Publications
2339 Venezia Drive
Davison, Michigan 48423

Printed in the United States of America

ISBN 0-923756-02-7

Other guidebooks by Friede Publications

A Traveler's Guide to 116 Michigan Lighthouses
Canoeing Michigan Rivers
Natural Michigan
A Guide to 199 Michigan Waterfalls
Michigan State and National Parks: A Complete Guide
Ultimate Michigan Adventures
Fish Michigan—100 Southern Michigan Lakes

For Barb, Chris and Joane, and Stephanie and Timm

ACKNOWLEDGMENTS

A book is never possible without the encouragement and expert assistance of an editor, publisher, layout artist, publicist, and creative consultant, all of which Gary Barfknecht of Friede Publications does with the ease of changing hats.

An appreciative thank you to the Nature Conservancy, the Little Traverse Conservancy, the Michigan Nature Association, the Michigan Audubon Society, and other organizations that fight to save our natural heritage.

And a special thank you to a long-time friend and sidekick, Dennis Banks, who made the long drives seem short and always knew north from south and east from west but rarely left from right.

All black-and-white photos are by Tom Powers and Barb Powers unless otherwise noted.

Photo, p. *ix:* Deerfield County Park (p. 83)
Photo, p. 158: Point Betsie Dunes Preserve (p. 72)

Cover Photos:

Front—Scotts Point (p. 24), by Dennis Banks
Back, top—Trail to Agate Beach (p. 1), by Barb Powers
Back, bottom—Purple Coneflower Preserve (p. 31), by Dennis Banks

The text of *More Natural Michigan* is printed on uncoated recycled paper.

INTRODUCTION

I never intended to write this book. With the publication of *Natural Michigan* in 1987, I knew that I hadn't exhausted the opportunities for enjoying the great natural splendor of our state, but in my naivete' I felt there probably just weren't enough other locations to warrant a sequel.

But over the years, readers of *Natural Michigan* stepped forward to suggest other natural attractions they thought deserved inclusion. And in my own travels I kept stumbling across fantastic but little-known gems of Michigan natural beauty.

When the list reached 50, I began serious research, which revealed even more remarkable places nature lovers could treasure in the state. Rare wet prairies, little-known botanical gardens, unique nature trails, awe-inspiring stretches of deserted Great Lake beaches, and even some California redwoods growing on a bluff overlooking Lake Michigan are just a sampling of the attractions you can find with the help of this book.

Repeating—but with even more emphasis—what I said in the introduction to *Natural Michigan*, we in Michigan are blessed, because within the borders of our state are almost numberless (though not always well-known) places at which we can enjoy quiet seclusion, unmatched natural beauty, and escape from the daily grind.

In *More Natural Michigan,* I'm pleased to present another 141 locations that hold our precious natural heritage.

Tom Powers
Flint, Michigan

SYMBOLS

🚶	HIKING	🎿	CROSS COUNTRY SKIING
🦆	BIRDWATCHING	⛺	CAMPING
🦋	NATURE STUDY	🚗	SCENIC DRIVE
⛱	PICNICKING	🏊	SWIMMING
📷	SCENIC ATTRACTION	⚓	HISTORICAL INTEREST

CONTENTS

UPPER PENINSULA

32

33

34

35

36

40

39

41 42 43

44 45

38

46 47 48

49

37

54 51 50

55 53 52

56 57 58 59

71

72

NORTHERN LOWER

73

60

68 69 68

74 75

61 62

63 64

76 70 67

65

77 66

78

79 80

81 82

84 86

85 87

83 108 109

110

111

88 89 112

113 114

90 91 115

SOUTHEASTERN
LOWER

92 101 116

117

128

103 127 126 119

102 104 105 120

106 107 125 121

129 124 123

SOUTHWESTERN
LOWER

130 131

100 133 132

134 135

136 137 138

96 99

97 98 141 140

139

95

93 94

118

122

LOWER PENINSULA

NORTHERN LOWER

SOUTHWESTERN LOWER

(continued on p. viii)

CONTENTS
(continued from p. vii)

SOUTHEASTERN LOWER

APPENDIXES

UPPER PENINSULA

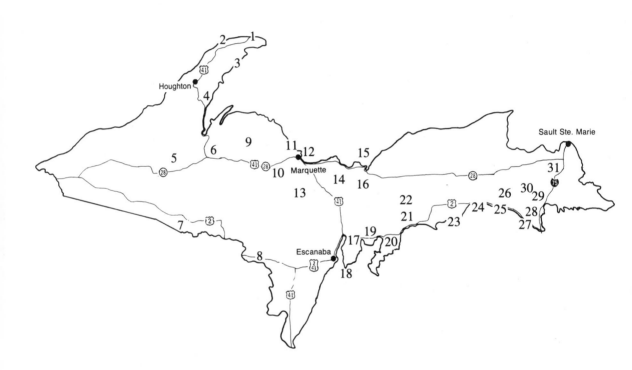

1   AGATE BEACH TRAIL

Amid the hustle and bustle of the major natural, historical and commercial attractions at Copper Harbor is a short hiking trail that you shouldn't miss. The half hour walk, which includes some unique views of this northern Michigan outpost, ends at one of the most dramatically beautiful beaches in the Keweenaw Peninsula, if not the state.

From the trailhead, at the west side of the Copper Harbor Marina, you slip into a primal northern forest as the path moves around the western end of the harbor. (Photo, back cover, top.) The trail is never far from the water as it cuts through the dense forest of coniferous trees, stunted by both the harsh northern winters and their exposed position near the lake. The trees are laden with moss and lichen, and in places the forest floor is thick with ferns. Turn your back to the forest, and you'll take in picturesque views of the little village across the bay.

After about three quarters of a mile, the trail forks. The right-hand path continues along the bay side of a long peninsula—which has sheltered Great Lakes shipping since the first schooner dropped anchor in 1843—and eventually ends at its tip, Hunter's Point.

The other path cuts across the narrow peninsula to Agate Beach, which absolutely wows first-time visitors. Huge chunks of bedrock—some of the world's oldest exposed rock—lie scattered across the beach. Conifers of all shapes and sizes line the edge of rock outcroppings that overlook the beach, and in some places the trees seem to have sprung whole from the living rock. Other smaller craggy outcroppings lie half buried in a vast cushion of small stones and pebbles that cover the shore. Look closely at the bedrock and you'll see delicately colored lichens plastered to it. More obvious is the array of wildflowers that grow out of pockets and fissures. Hidden among the millions of stones and pebbles that line the beach are prized Lake Superior agates, and the entire area is a treasure trove for beachcombers and rockhounds.

County/City: Keweenaw/Copper Harbor

Fees: None.

Schedule: Open all year.

Directions: The trail begins at the Copper Harbor Marina parking lot, on the west side of town.

Upper Peninsula

2 M-26

The slender ribbon of asphalt that hugs the rock-bound northern coastline of the Keweenaw Peninsula between Copper Harbor and Eagle River ranks as one of the most beautiful scenic drives in the Great Lakes.

For most of the 14-mile distance between the two small villages, M-26 dips and turns like a miniature roller coaster along shoreline that seems totally out of place in Michigan. Only yards from the shoulder of the road, huge slabs of darkly colored bedrock—sculpted by wind and waves into long, bony fingers that parallel the highway—tilt into the sparkling water of Lake Superior. At other spots the canted, aging rock rears into the air before plunging into the lake.

Scattered along the drive are four stops you shouldn't miss—two Michigan Nature Association preserves (identified by small "protected area" signs), a waterfall, and a roadside park.

At an MNA preserve 4.5 miles south of Copper Harbor, you can park on the highway's wide shoulder and explore the unique rock formations that dip into Lake Superior. When you climb over the rugged shoreline, you may be astounded to find life struggling for existence in the extraordinary environment. Beautiful flowers sprout from small cracks in the rock; many-colored lichen appears wedded to the stone; and gnarled, stunted trees—natural bonsai that have been shaped by the elements—cling precariously to the rock.

About four miles farther south, another MNA preserve and an adjacent roadside park present two strikingly different vistas. At the roadside park, several picnic tables are sheltered behind a huge, craggy rock dome that compels you to climb to its top for a sweeping view of Lake Superior. Just west, the MNA preserve borders both sides of the road, but it's the landward side that calls for attention. There, a faint but posted hiking trail slips into an enchanted forest, where trees drip with lichen and nearly every rock and downed tree is covered by a deep cushion of moss.

Another mile or so south, M-26 crosses the Silver River. Practically from the exact point where the road bridges the stream, the water plunges toward the lake in a series of drops called Silver River Falls. You can't see the falls from your car, but it's a short, easy climb from a parking lot beside the bridge down the slope for a great view.

From Silver River it's 4.5 miles to Eagle River, and along that stretch of the road, Lake Superior is seldom seen as M-26 tunnels through a pristine forest and borders a picturesque inland lake.

County/City: Keweenaw/Copper Harbor
Fees: None.
Schedule: Open all year.
Directions: Drive south on M-26 from Copper Harbor.

3 KEWEENAW BAY SHORELINE DRIVE

Visitors to the uniquely scenic Keweenaw Peninsula are mesmerized by the beauty of its northern shoreline. The county's only major roads, US-41 and M-26 (see p. 2), parallel the north side of the peninsula, and there's so much to see and do along those two highways that most tourists never think to explore Keweenaw's south side. They should. The neglected 20-mile-long blacktop road that runs between Gay and Lac La Belle along the edge of Lake Superior holds half a day's worth of beautiful and unusual scenery, all of which you can enjoy without leaving your car.

Beginning at Gay, on the south end of the drive, the road slips through the forest that borders the big lake, and you get only intermittent views of the water. Just when you begin to get frustrated with the peek-a-boo glimpses of Superior, the road reaches Burnette Bay Park, about seven miles north of Gay.

At that roadside park, a sandy swimming beach dips into the chilly waters of the great lake, and a few scattered picnic tables line the beach. But it's the magnificent view of Superior that demands your immediate attention. To the east, the deep blue-green water stretches to the horizon, and 30 miles across the water to the south rise the outlines of the Huron Mountains. You can take in the entire scene without leaving your vehicle, but the sandy shoreline has an almost irresistible pull and most travelers walk the shore and even wade in the bracingly cool water.

Continuing on the drive north from the roadside park, more-frequent views of the lake and Huron Mountains will keep your head turned to the right. Just before the road veers away from the shoreline and cuts cross-country to Lac La Belle, a breathtaking view of Bette Grise Bay and the eastern tip of the Keweenaw Peninsula pulls drivers to the side of the road for a final and memorable look.

From there the road cuts west, away from the shoreline, through a dense northern forest before reaching Lac La Belle. On the outskirts of the tiny

village is a final reward—a lovely roadside park with a picture-perfect waterfall and picnic area. You can easily see Haven Falls from the road, but you really shouldn't pass up the opportunity to park and more closely explore the curtain of water pouring over a near-20-foot-tall, sheer wall of rock. The small picnic area is deeply shaded, and the falls takes center stage at this natural version of a dinner theater.

County/City: Keweenaw/Gay
Fees: None.
Schedule: Open all year.
Directions: Drive north from Gay.

4 STURGEON RIVER SLOUGHS WATERFOWL AREA

The Sturgeon River Sloughs Waterfowl Area catches many Keweenaw Peninsula visitors off guard. Most of us expect dramatic or at least clearly defined meetings of land and water in the remote, rugged area. So when driving US-41 south of Houghton, it can come as a surprise when the highway passes a vast wetlands created by the Sturgeon River as it flows into Portage Lake.

The waterfowl area encompasses a huge diked flood plain and vast marsh, most of which can be seen from the top of an observation deck just off US-41 at the back of a gravel parking lot. When you climb the nearly two-story tower, you'll be convinced you are seeing the flattest stretch of real estate in the entire peninsula. Drainage ditches etch the fields close at hand, but in the distance the only evidence of the ditches are slight folds in the marsh's grand expanse of waving grass. Binoculars are a must if you want to search out distant Great Blue Herons or catch a glimpse of a Sand-hill Crane.

Adjacent to the observation deck, the three-mile Bert DeVriendt Nature Trail slips through a gate in a fence and then follows the top of the dikes that circle the waterfowl area. The woodchip-covered trail passes the brushy fringes of channels alongside the dikes, reed-choked marshes, and open fields, all of which offer good birding opportunities nearly any time of the year. Beaver, mink, muskrat and raccoon also inhabit the area, and interpretive signs along the path tell of the history of the natural area and the flora and fauna usually found on the hike.

County/City: Houghton/Chassel

Fees: None.

Schedule: Open all year.

Directions: From Houghton drive 7 miles south on US-41.

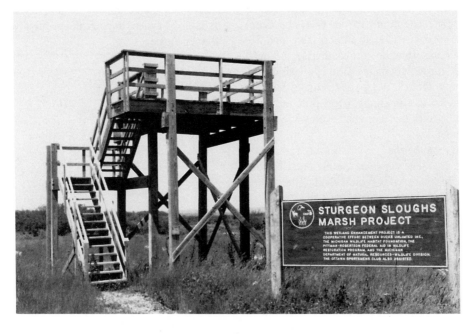

5 STURGEON RIVER GORGE WILDERNESS AREA

The heart of this spectacular wilderness area in the Ottawa National Forest is, as the Forest Service describes it, "the deepest readily accessible gorge east of the Mississippi." Michigan's "Grand Canyon" is a 250- to 300-foot-deep, one-half- to one-mile-wide trench carved out of the Upper Peninsula's high, rolling landscape by the swift-moving Sturgeon River. But "readily accessible" must be qualified. The gorge is surrounded by 14,139 acres of wilderness, and to get the most-stunning views, you have to drive nearly 10 miles on a narrow forest road, then do some strenuous hiking. But it's worth the side trip and the exercise, because the gorge is a one-of-a-kind experience in the Midwest.

For day-trippers the most popular destination (and by popular I'm not talking Disneyland crowds, but maybe one or two other people a day) is the hike down into the forest-shrouded gorge to see Sturgeon Falls. Depending on road conditions, it's anywhere from a half-mile to a mile hike down an old two-track. The road falls over the side of the gorge, then parallels the river high above the water. The scenery is fantastic as the trail slowly descends to just above a long series of falls, the last of which, Sturgeon, is a 40-foot drop through a narrow chute.

From Forest Road 2200, which borders the east side of the gorge and wilderness area, you get occasional panoramic views of the green-clad canyon. The road descends into the valley about five miles north of M-26, and as it crosses a one-lane bridge, you get a marvelous view of the boiling water. On the north side of the river, the road climbs the steep valley wall and then borders the gorge for several miles. Turnoffs, old two-tracks closed to vehicles, and foot trails break off from the road and head toward the gorge.

There are no marked or formal trails and no campgrounds within the wilderness area, but you are free to wander throughout the rugged, heavily wooded terrain. Be sure to take a compass and write for a map of the area if you plan an extended outing. You can backcountry camp throughout the area or also set up at a small, picturesque national forest campground just outside the wilderness area at the point where FR-2200 crosses the river.

County/City: Houghton and Baraga/Sidnaw

Fees: None.

Schedule: Open all year if roads are passable.

Directions: Forest Rd. 2200 is shown on state highway maps as a broken gray line heading north from M-28 just east of Sidnaw. The wilderness area begins about 3 miles north of M-28 and is on the west side of FR-2200.

To reach the trail to Sturgeon Falls, drive 12.9 miles north of M-26 on FR-2200 to FR-2270. Turn left (west) onto FR-2270 and drive 0.9 miles to a two-track that enters from the left. The trailhead is 1/2 mile down the track.

Further Information: Ottawa National Forest, Kenton Ranger District, Kenton, MI 49943.

6 ABRAMSON ROADSIDE PARK

The grand expanse of Upper Peninsula wilderness can sometimes be too overpowering to fully take in or experience. It's the old saw of not being able to see the forest for the trees. But within an easy hundred-yard stroll at this postage-stamp-size roadside park, you get a wonderful slice of western UP beauty that's easy to digest and appreciate.

The park nestles in a bend of Tioga Creek, right next to Michigan highway M-28. Picnic tables and grills lie scattered across a grassy meadow on the inside of the creek's loop and only a few feet from a small waterfall, whose copper-colored water tumbles over a series of small, rocky ledges and boulders. The low, rhythmic rumble of the falls adds background music to any roadside repast. Just below the boiling water, you get good views

of the falls and creek from a footbridge that leads to a few more picnic tables on the outside of the creek's bend.

From the larger picnic area, a woodchip-covered trail follows the creek upstream through a narrow forested valley to a second, slightly larger falls. Several towering old-growth white pines, which somehow escaped the lumbermen's axes, line the trail and cast their shadows over the strikingly beautiful valley and swift-moving water. At the end of the trail, the second waterfall pours over a bedrock outcropping into a quiet pool. Most visitors make the brief walk to the falls, take in the scene, then leave without realizing that just above the falls and visible from the end of the well-worn path is a beaver dam.

Faint trails wind through the woods around the falls to a memorable view of the quiet pond that's backed by deep-green pines and necklaced with silent wetlands and dead trees killed by the flooding. You can creep to within a few feet of the beaver dam and also walk along barely discernable trails that head off along the edge of the pond.

County/City: Baraga/Three Lakes
Fees: None.
Schedule: None.
Directions: From the junction of M-28 and US-41, go 6.5 miles east on M-28.

7 STATELINE NATIONAL RECREATION TRAIL

This short, pleasant and scenic Ottawa National Forest trail marks the starting point of the only state boundary line in the Upper Peninsula that isn't water. The trail begins at a small picnic grounds at the south end of Brule Lake. From near there, at the headwaters of the Brule River, the boundary between Wisconsin and Michigan heads overland northwest almost 70 miles to the Montreal River, south of Ironwood. An interpretive sign at the start of the pathway explains the significance of the area and the work of the surveyors in laying out the boundary.

From the interpretive sign, the trail runs south along the edge of the Brule River a third of a mile through a picturesque hardwood forest to the Mile Post Zero survey monument, which marks the exact starting point of the overland boundary line. Another third of a mile downriver, the trail ends at the Treaty Tree Site. There, an interpretive sign and the time-weathered stump of the treaty tree sit on the spot where two pacts were signed with area Indians in order to safeguard the surveyors as they ran the boundary line.

Facilities at the small picnic area at the trailhead include five tables and grills, a well, pit toilets, and a boat launching ramp onto Brule Lake.

County/City: Iron/Iron River

Fees: None.

Schedule: None posted, but it's best to go during summer months only.

Directions: From Iron River go west on US-2 2.5 miles to M-73. Turn left (southwest) onto M-73 and go 5 miles to Hagerman Lake Rd. Turn right (north) onto Hagerman and drive 2 miles to West Brule Lake Rd. Turn left (west) onto W. Brule and go 2 miles to a north-south road junction. Turn hard left (south) and drive one mile to the picnic area.

8 PIERS GORGE SCENIC AREA

The Menominee River's tortuous run through Piers Gorge—just south of Norway, Michigan—marks the most magically beautiful point along the entire Michigan/Wisconsin border. The Menominee forms the longest river boundary in Michigan and makes up nearly a third of the state line on the western end of the Upper Peninsula. The rust-colored, swiftly moving river is beautiful anywhere along its length, but the scenery is simply spectacular at Piers Gorge, where the water is dramatically funneled through steep-sided rock walls and forced over a succession of stony shelves.

The gorge's walls, which rise as high as 70 feet above the river, twist and turn like an amusement-park water slide. In places, only bare bedrock guards the penned-in water, but more often, trees cling to the near-vertical walls and soften the view. Four separate waterfalls, each with its own distinct character, send the river into tumultuous descents. They are cheated of some of their glamour by the almost continuous rapids that kick up white water and create a roar throughout the river's journey through the gorge.

You can take in memorable views of all four falls and the rapids from a trail—first used by Indians to portage their canoes around the falls—that follows the top of the gorge. The level, easily walked path begins at a parking lot at the end of Piers Gorge Road and crosses a small cedar swamp before slipping through a mature northern forest of hardwoods and pine. Offshoots from the trail snake out to the edge of the gorge, and others creep down the steep slope to the very edge of the churning water. A three-mile round trip along the top of the gorge to all the falls can take more than an hour and several rolls of film.

County/City: Dickinson/Norway

Fees: None.

Schedule: Open all year.

Directions: From US-2 in Norway, drive 2 miles south on US-8. About 1/4 mile before crossing the bridge into Wisconsin, turn right (west) onto Piers Gorge Rd. and drive 1/2 mile to the parking lot.

9 MCCORMICK WILDERNESS TRACT

🚶 ⛷ ⛺

Even a quick glance at a state highway map suggests the remoteness of this 27-square-mile area of pristine wilderness. Go on, get out the map, look at the Upper Peninsula and trace US-41 from Marquette west to L'Anse. About halfway between those two towns, and the width of a thumb north of Lake Michigamme, sits the rugged, isolated and scenic McCormick Wilderness Tract. As the map indicates, this area is nearly smack dab in the middle of one of the state's largest expanses of wilderness.

The property served as a vacation retreat for the Cyrus McCormick family, of reaping machine fame, until the 1967 death of Gordon McCormick, who willed the estate to the National Forest Service. The McCormick family kept much of the land from being lumbered, and as a result, impressive stands of white pine grow on many areas of the property. Other sections of the preserve haven't been logged for over 70 years, and a lush second-growth forest covers the once-cut-over land.

Don't let the fact that this place was once the playground of the rich and famous mislead you into thinking it's user-friendly. This is not Cannes or Vail. This is a wilderness of high hills, deep forests, rambunctious rivers, rocky cliffs, primeval lakes, rough bedrock outcroppings, and vast muskegs, all devoid of any but the faintest trails. The land is so remote and little-visited that two waterfalls—East Falls and North Falls, which drops 140 feet in an eighth of a mile—not generally listed in even the most comprehensive guides to Michigan waterfalls, hide in the preserve.

"Easy" can hardly if ever be used to describe the hiking conditions here. Foot trails and paths at one time webbed the tract, but those old routes, used by the long-ago McCormicks, have become overgrown and most have all but disappeared. Except for a three-mile-long foot trail that connects County Road 607 to White Deer Lake, where the family estate once stood, hikers have to blaze their own way into the wilderness. The U.S. Forest Ser-

vice recommends that you take a U.S. Geological Survey Quadrangle Map (available from the address below), a compass, and a survival kit for even a day trip here. It's rough going and not for the novice, but the exertion and hardship pay off in equal rewards—the chance to enjoy waterfalls few people even know exist; a rugged, unspoiled wilderness; more solitude than most hermits experience; spectacular views of the Huron Mountains to the north; and likely spottings of moose, Pine Martin and beaver.

You can backcountry camp throughout the area, but leave no trace of your passing. And before camping here, write or visit the Kenton Ranger Office for detailed maps, camping techniques, and local road conditions. Cross country skiers are welcome, but winters here can be brutal, with fast-changing weather and road conditions. Go prepared and don't go alone.

County/City: Marquette/Champion

Fees: None.

Schedule: Open all year.

Directions: From US-41 just west of Champion, drive 12 miles north on County Rd. 607 (Huron Bay Grade).

Further Information: Kenton Ranger District, Ottawa National Forest, Kenton, MI 49943.

Upper Peninsula

10   BLACK RIVER PATHWAY

Beautiful Black River Falls serves as the official greeter at this Escanaba State Forest pathway. It's a short, easy walk from the parking lot to the 20-foot-tall cascade of copper-colored water, which marks the stepping-off point for nine miles of trails that wind through an open pine forest. Before you embark on a hike, be sure to cross the short footbridge that connects to an island at the base of the falls. From the island, which divides the flow after its plunge from the rocky cliff, you get a striking head-on view of the airborne river.

Away from the falls, the pathway traverses flat to hilly terrain, crosses the Black River upstream from the waterfall, slips past quiet Sleeman Pond, follows an old logging road, and at its farthest reach, offers a scenic overlook of the Middle Branch of the Escanaba River. Benches are conveniently spaced along the trail.

A 1986 forest fire obliterated several parts of the pathway. Prior to the fire, four loops, from 1.1 to 7.7 miles long, ranged through the picturesque landscape, but temporary rerouting of the pathway has wiped out one of the shortest loops. Though an inconvenience, it's also an excellent chance to study how forests recover from fires.

Cross country skiers are welcome to use the pathway in the winter.

County/City: Marquette/Ishpeming

Fees: None.

Schedule: Open all year.

Directions: Southwest of Ishpeming, take County Rd. 581 (also called Saginaw St.) 8 miles to Island Lake Rd. Turn right (west) onto Island and drive 1/2 mile to the trailhead.

11 SUGAR LOAF MOUNTAIN PATHWAY

From the peak of Sugar Loaf Mountain, you can take in the most spectacular and memorable view of the Lake Superior coastline to be had between the Pictured Rocks and the Keweenaw Peninsula. But you'll probably be tired when you do.

It doesn't seem like it should be much of a climb. From its starting point to the top of the mountain, Sugar Loaf Mountain Pathway gains only 315 feet in elevation. That's barely more than a football field turned on end. But to the seriously out of shape and those who generally forego stairs in favor of elevators, legs will be quivering and lungs bursting by the end of the hike.

The trail starts gradually from the parking lot, ascending through a beautiful birch and mixed evergreen forest. But just when it lulls you into thinking, "Gee this is an easy walk," the trail hits a seemingly endless series of staircases. Sixteen separate flights of stairs, to be exact, that circle around or climb right up the face of huge rock outcroppings. Moss and ferns cover the aging bedrock, and gnarled, old trees cling for life to it.

The final flight of stairs takes you to the top of the nearly bald dome of rock and panoramic views from three separate observation platforms. Marquette Harbor, to the east, looks like a model train layout; the green humps to the west make it easy to imagine you're in the Appalachian Mountains; and to the north stretches the great expanse of the world's largest freshwater sea.

You can get even more exercise and stunning beauty by following the trail that heads north along the shoreline from the top of the mountain. A one-mile hike will take you to Wetmore Landing, and 1.6 miles farther, the trail ends at Little Presque Isle. The terrain is rough and hilly, and you will climb and descend many more flights of stairs.

County/City: Marquette/Marquette

Fees: None.

Schedule: Open all year.

Directions: Drive 5 miles north of Marquette on County Rd. 550.

Upper Peninsula

12 PRESQUE ISLE PARK

Presque Isle Park offers the most striking scenery of any city park in the Upper Peninsula, and maybe the state. From the 328-acre peninsula, which curls out into Lake Superior on the northwest side of Marquette, you get knockout views of the great lake, Marquette Harbor, and rugged shoreline at every turn of your head.

A narrow, one-way blacktop road that circles the peninsula alternates between slipping through a dense northern forest and edging the coastline, where panoramic views of the lake slow motorists to a crawl. At several turnouts you can stop and admire the scenery or leave your car for walks on numerous short trails that lead to overlooks of the peninsula's towering cliffs, sand beaches and ancient rock outcroppings. In the evening the most popular spot in the park is Sunset Point, at the north end of the peninsula, where the sun's descent into the lake rarely fails to beguile.

If you'd prefer to explore the park on foot, nature and hiking trails also eventually arrive at all points of interest, including some that motorists can't reach.

You can picnic at two different areas. One grassy site, just inside the park entrance, covers the southern tip of the peninsula and overlooks

Lake Superior and the busy harbor. Tables and grills at another picnic grounds line a sandy swimming beach along the west shore of the park. The shallow, protected bay formed by the peninsula is as warm a swimming spot as you can find in Lake Superior, and the wide expanse of sand will have sand castle builders breaking out shovels, trowels and buckets. If you don't want to brave the big lake's chilly waters, you can jump into a swimming pool, Michigan's largest, near the park entrance.

Other facilities here include tennis courts, a 160-foot water slide, a small zoo featuring a herd of whitetail deer, a park store, and in the winter, extensive cross country ski trails.

Also, from a public viewing area near the giant Lake Superior and Ishpeming Railroad Ore Dock, just outside the park entrance, you can get close-up looks at huge ore boats being loaded with taconite.

County/City: Marquette/Marquette

Fees: None.

Schedule: Open all year.

Directions: On the west side of Marquette, follow Lakeshore Blvd. to the park entrance.

13 ANDERSON LAKE PATHWAY

On Anderson Lake Pathway's four loops, hikers and cross country skiers can tour the heart of the Escanaba River State Forest. Ranging in length from 2.0 to 4.3 miles, the loops cross rolling to hilly terrain covered with beautiful stands of hardwoods and pines. Three small lakes, marshes, and scattered interpretive signs, which point out the area's natural features and history, add interest and variety to any trek.

The pathway begins at a 19-site state forest campground, which is strung out along the west shore of Anderson Lake. The quiet, secluded campground makes an excellent base from which to explore both the trail system and the few forest roads that pierce the remote and scenic state forest land. The sandy swimming beach next to the campground is a good spot to cool off weary feet, or more if you like. And there's a boat launch onto the lake, which holds out possibilities for good catches of bass, perch, pike and bluegills.

Three of the pathway's four loops are suitable for cross country skiing and progress in difficulty from beginner through advanced. The road into the campground is not plowed in the winter, so you have to ski the access road to get to the trails.

County/City: Marquette/Gwinn

Fees: None.

Schedule: Open all year.

Directions: From Gwinn, drive 7 miles south on County Rd. 557.

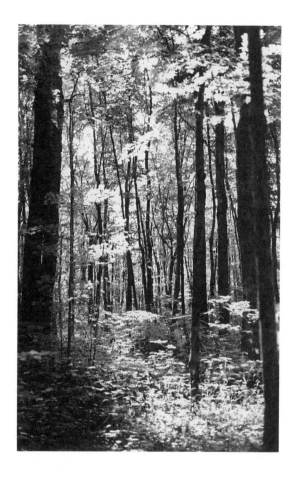

Upper Peninsula

14 ROCK RIVER CANYON WILDERNESS AREA

Two canyons, cut more than 150 feet deep into the Upper Peninsula's sandstone bedrock, are the highlight at this remote corner of the Hiawatha National Forest.

The wilderness area surrounding the canyons was extensively logged between the late 1800s and 1930, and a second-growth forest of northern hardwoods now covers the plateau through which the Rock River and Silver Creek have sculpted deep, parallel grooves that look like they could be ruts from the giant wagon pulled by Paul Bunyan's blue ox, Babe.

The canyons themselves have remained relatively undisturbed by humans. Their floors are wet and dense with vegetation, and their walls are interrupted by caves and a beautiful waterfall. At the canyons' edges, water and weather have worked at the sandstone outcropping and fashioned openings 10 to 40 feet deep in the soft rock. In the winter, water seeps over the canyon walls, freezes, and forms spectacular ice curtains that hang in front of the caves. Waterfall lovers will want to add Rock River Falls—described as one of the most beautiful and remote in Alger County—to the list of those they have seen and photographed. The Rock River takes a 20-foot leap off a sandstone ledge and dives into a dark, quiet pool.

Getting down into the canyons over their rough walls is, at best, difficult. But an unmatched sense of personal solitude and a chance to explore the unique scenery and terrain are the payoffs for the strenuous climb.

Hiking in the rest of wilderness area is easier, since most of the 5,343-acre preserve is relatively flat and easily walked. Old logging roads, skid trails, and two abandoned railroad grades provide access, but there are no marked trails. If you plan an extended hike or overnight backpacking trip here, you should write for a detailed topographical map, available for $1 from the Hiawatha National Forest, address below.

The area is bounded on the east and west by Forest roads 2279, 2276 and 2293, and several jumping-off places are scattered along those narrow roads. For a good taste of the area and the shortest route to an overlook of Rock River Canyon and Falls, take Rock River Road north out of Chatham and drive 4.3 miles to USFS 2276. Turn left (west) onto 2276 and drive 4.3 miles to a small, marked parking area. A 3/4-mile-long trail leads downhill from the parking lot to the falls and canyon.

Also worth seeing is Ginpole Lake, near the southern edge of the preserve. The shallow, secluded lake rests in the bottom of Rock River Canyon, and sandstone walls rise sharply from the water's edge. Fishermen with the tenacity and stamina to scramble down to the water can test their skill and luck against the rainbow trout, brook trout, brown trout, coho salmon and northern pike that inhabit the picturesque lake.

County/City: Alger/Chatham

Fees: None.

Schedule: Open all year.

Directions: In Chatham where M-94 makes a sharp turn west, drive north on Rock River Rd. (H-01) for 2 miles. For the next 1.6 miles, the wilderness area is on your immediate left. At the junction with FR-2276, turn left. For the next 5 miles, the wilderness area borders the left side of the road.

Further Information: Forest Supervisor, Hiawatha National Forest, 2727 N. Lincoln Rd., Escanaba, MI 49829.

15 GRAND ISLAND

🚶 📷 ⛺ 🏛

In 1657 Pierre Radisson, the first European to visually embrace the odd-shaped chunk of land plopped into Lake Superior just a half mile from the shoreline near (present-day) Munising, called Grand Island a "terrestrial paradise." Since then no one has argued with his description, and most visitors come away from a trip to the eight-mile-long, three-mile-wide island agreeing that nature has created one of the most beautiful spots in the world.

The trouble was that, until recently, few people had a chance to enjoy the second-largest of the Lake Superior islands that lie in American waters. The Cleveland Cliffs Iron Company bought the island in 1901 and used it as a private hunting preserve and corporate retreat for the next 89 years. That all changed in 1990, when the federal government purchased Grand Island for 3.4 million dollars and designated it as a National Recreation Area.

Plans for future use and the number and kinds of facilities will probably remain unclear until the

(Continued on p. 16)

Flint Public Library Photo File

Upper Peninsula

GRAND ISLAND

(Continued from p. 15)

next century, but you shouldn't wait to visit. Right now, you have free run of almost the entire island, and it's not going to get any prettier. The country's westernmost stand of virgin beech trees plus white pine the equal of or even larger than those at Hartwick Pines State Park grow here. One-mile-long Echo Lake, near the center of the island, is the largest beaver pond in the world. Caves and waterfalls not listed in even the best of guidebooks dot the island, and bears, coyotes, beaver, grouse, loons and an occasional eagle grace the land, water and sky.

But it's the island's spectacular 35-mile-long shoreline that will leave you with the most lasting impressions and will convince you of the rightness of the island's name. Sheer 200-foot sandstone walls have been sculpted by wind and battered by waves and ice into a scenic marvel that rivals the

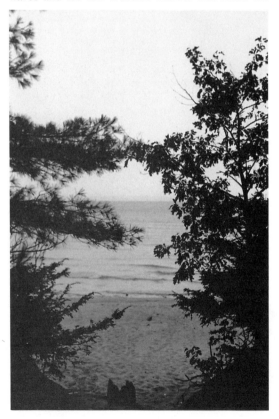

world-renowned Pictured Rocks National Lakeshore, just across Munising Bay. The park service is currently developing a lakeshore trail, that will allow full exploration of the unusual scenery, and other footpaths already lace the island's interior.

You can camp anywhere on public land (18 summer cottages and two lighthouses remain in private hands), but be warned that in May and June black flies can make life miserable.

Grand Island's history is as fascinating as its scenery. The island stumps geologists. They can explain the formation and existence of all the world's islands except this one. Maybe the Indian legend is right. Chippewas who lived here believed that the Great Spirit, having nothing else to do, began creating giants. But the Spirit lost interest and, instead of giving the giants life, threw one into Lake Superior. Grand Island is that giant's body, and two smaller islands to the west, Williams and Wood, are the giant's hands. The Great Spirit threw the other giants onto the mainland, where they became the hills of Munising.

The Chippewas lived on the island well into the 19th century, and Europeans had settled here by the 1840s. The first two houses built by Europeans still stand, as do two picturesque lighthouses erected in 1867. Both lighthouses are privately owned and not open to the public.

County/City: Alger/Munising

Fees: Fare for a Pictured Rocks Cruises boat trip to and from the island is $7 round trip.

Schedule: The island is open all year. Pictured Rock Cruises makes two trips to the island daily in the summer. Call or write for a current schedule. Also, it may be possible to reach the island during the winter by snowmobile or possibly skis.

Directions: To get to Pictured Rocks Cruises, in Munising from where M-28 makes a 90-degree turn, go west on M-28 1/4 mile to Elm St. Turn right, onto Elm, and go 2 blocks.

Further Information: Hiawatha National Forest, Munising Ranger District, 400 E. Munising Ave., Munising, MI 49862.

Pictured Rocks Cruises, P.O. Box 355, Munising, MI 49862; (906) 387-2379.

16   BRUNO'S RUN HIKING TRAIL

Winding through a maze of picturesque lakes scattered across the heart of Hiawatha National Forest, the 7.5-mile-long Bruno's Run Hiking Trail offers hikers and backpackers anywhere from a challenging one-day hike to a leisurely two- or three-day trek amid striking landscape.

Though it can be done, most hikers have trouble maintaining a fast enough pace to close the circle in a single day. It's not that the walking is difficult, but rather there is just too much natural beauty to hurry past. The pathway touches nine different lakes and crosses several sparkling streams, and its southern section runs over low foothills dotted with scenic overlooks. Between Fish and Moccasin lakes, the trail follows an old logging grade and penetrates a stand of mature hemlocks so imposing they bear the name Hemlock Cathedral. And if you stay alert and move with a minimum of noise, you have excellent chances of spotting the area's abundant wildlife.

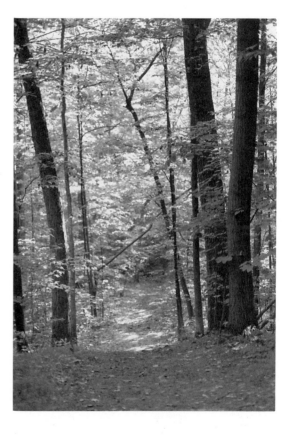

The trail passes two national forest campgrounds. Hiking clockwise from the main trailhead at Moccasin Lake, the campground at Pete's Lake is 1.3 miles down the trail. The sites at Widewater Campground are about a mile walk counterclockwise from the same trailhead. Backcountry camping is also allowed anywhere along the route.

A map, available from the National Forest's Munising Ranger District, shows the length of each stage of the trail and also the location of several access points. The easiest-reached trailhead is on the north end of the loop at Moccasin Lake next to a small picnic grounds.

County/City: Schoolcraft/Wetmore

Fees: None.

Schedule: Open all year.

Directions: From Wetmore, drive 11 miles south on H-13.

Further Information: Hiawatha National Forest, Munising Ranger District, Munising, MI 49826.

Upper Peninsula

17 SQUAW CREEK OLD GROWTH AREA

A walk through the Squaw Creek Old Growth Area is a journey back in time. Take just a few steps off County Road 513, and you can't help but feel what the state's great forests must have looked like before the lumbering era.

The 65-acre preserve doesn't contain a stand of virgin timber, because several thinnings occurred prior to 1940, when the area was added to the Hiawatha National Forest. But when loggers worked this area in the late 1800s, a significant number of large trees were left untouched, and they have grown into magnificent specimens. Today, you can hike beneath towering white pine, hemlocks, huge hardwoods and red pine, the smallest of which are telephone-pole size.

Old Squaw Creek, which cuts across the southern half of the old-growth area, adds its own special charm to the scenery. The fast-moving, red-tinged creek flows between high banks that twist and turn through the woods like a partially uncoiled spring. Huge trees grow along the banks and in many places tilt toward each other from opposite shores to form a green tent over the cool water.

There are no marked trails, but old two-tracks and narrow, overgrown roads—closed to all but foot traffic—penetrate to every corner of the hushed, pine-scented woods. Walking is easy over the needle-soft trails, and the lack of a dense understory in many places invites you to wander at will among trees that will dwarf you. If you plan to hike to the far reaches of the tract or if you like to blaze your own trail through the woods, be sure to take a compass.

County/City: Delta/Rapid River

Fees: None.

Schedule: Open all year.

Directions: From Rapid River, drive 2.5 miles east on US-2 to County Rd. 513. Turn right (south) onto CR-513 and go 9 miles to Squaw Creek. The old-growth area is on the east side of the road, and you can park at several pulloffs on either side of the creek.

18 PENINSULA POINT LIGHTHOUSE PARK

🚶 🏕 📷

In a state made up of so many peninsulas, the finger of land that juts out into Lake Michigan to separate Big and Little Bays De Noc is often forgotten or ignored. Except for a private campground, the seldom-visited peninsula is nearly devoid of commercial tourist attractions. But the 18-mile drive from US-2 to its tip, called Peninsula Point, is well worth the time and gas for anyone who treasures little-visited, out-of-the-way scenery or an unusual picnic spot.

A pleasant, grass-covered picnic grounds surrounds the remains of an old lighthouse at land's end. From the open, sunny meadow, you get great views of Lake Michigan in three directions. Visible five miles across Little Bay De Noc (but 35 miles away by car) is the city of Escanaba. And south from the tip of the peninsula, you look right down the throat of Green Bay. Only the foundation of the lightkeeper's house remains, but the light tower is still standing and you can climb to its top on an iron corkscrew stairway to a sweeping view of the green shores that trace the distant edge of the vast expanse of water.

The shoreline—flat slabs of bedrock that reach out into the lake—isn't good for swimming. But beachcombers will delight in poking around in the ankle-deep water, examining driftwood captured by the point, and turning over an occasional odd rock.

On the western side of the peninsula, a short nature/hiking trail heads north along the shore, then turns inland. For the first few hundred yards, as it cuts through a thick woods fringing Big Bay De Noc, the path is rarely out of sight and sound of the wave-lapped shore. When the trail curls inland, it crosses a quiet cedar swamp, where you slip over wet areas on a boardwalk. The last quarter mile of the trail turns back south and joins the narrow one-lane road leading to the tip of the point.

County/City: Delta/Stonington

Fees: None.

Schedule: Open all year.

Directions: Go 18 miles south of US-2 on County Rd. 513.

19 STURGEON RIVER

In its last 17-mile serpentine march to Lake Michigan, the Sturgeon River passes through a section of the Hiawatha National Forest notable for its untamed beauty and ease of access. Because of its pristine condition and the beautiful landscape—vast pine and hardwood forests, huge cedar swamps and black-spruce bogs—it winds through before emptying into Big Bay De Noc, the Sturgeon has been nominated under the Michigan Natural Rivers Act for designation as a Wild-Scenic River. It's easy, both literally and figuratively, to see why. If you catch even a glimpse of the swiftly flowing stream as it disappears around one of its ever-present bends, it will stay fixed in your mind. And you don't have to drive miles out of your way over two-tracks or hike through rough country to experience its grandeur.

From US-2, heading southeast from Nahma Junction, County Road 497 borders the west bank of the river for five miles to the head of Big Bay De Noc. The paved road is more patches than original blacktop, which is no problem because it helps you take your time and enjoy the sights. Though rarely far from the road, the river weaves in and out of view because it is usually screened by the lush pine and hardwood forest. You can get closer looks from several pulloffs where you can park and explore on foot.

Wildlife abounds in the area, and it would be rare not to spot a grouse, skunk, raccoon, porcupine or other animal crossing the road.

At Nahma, where the Sturgeon slides into Lake Michigan, County Road 497 junctions with County Road 499. You can head back to US-2 by turning west onto 499, and if you do, you will take in entirely different scenery. On its seven-mile loop back, the old blacktop edges the shallow, grassy shoreline of Lake Michigan. This is not the dramatic meeting of land and water we've come to expect along the lake, but rather an almost indistinct merging of the two elements. On the water side of the low dunes, the barely sloping sand

makes a long run to meet Lake Michigan. Beach grasses cover much of the area and reach out into the lake, which gives the impression that a vast wetlands is slowly rising from the water. You can pull over at several turnouts along the road and explore the miles of fascinating shoreline on foot.

County/City: Delta/Nahma
Fees: None.
Schedule: Open all year.
Directions: From Nahma Junction turn south onto County Rd. 497.

20 NINGA AKI PATHWAY

🚶 🦋 📷 ⛺

How native Americans used sphagnum moss as America's first disposable diaper, made tea from white-pine needles to cure sore throats, and splinted broken bones with birch bark are only a few of the fascinating bits of Indian lore you'll learn along the Ninga Aki Pathway.

Located on the aptly named Garden Peninsula, the interpretive trail takes you through a quiet, picturesque section of the Lake Superior State Forest and also back in time to when native Americans depended entirely on nature for food, clothing, medicine and building materials. Ninga Aki means "Mother Earth" in the Ojibwa tongue, and at 15 numbered stops along the trail, you'll discover just how important the forest resources were to every aspect of the Indians' daily lives. They used ground juniper berries, thimbleberries, balsam fir, aspen seeds, brackens, the inner bark from dogwood, and numerous other plants for everything from reducing a fever to making bread dough to lashing together a wigwam.

The short, easily walked trail begins at the 18-site Portage Bay State Forest Campground, which hugs the bay and looks out over the vast expanse of Lake Michigan. In addition to hiking, campers here can also swim from a fine beach that fronts the campsites or fish for bass, perch, bluegill and pike in the bay's sheltered waters. The campground also serves as a great base for exploring the unspoiled beauty of the Garden Peninsula. The out-of-the way finger of land has miles of beautiful shoreline, lonely and picturesque backcountry roads, and a quaint fishing village near its tip.

County/City: Delta/Garden

Fees: None for trail use.

Schedule: Open summer months only.

Directions: From the village of Garden, drive south on County Rd. 483 approximately 17 miles to Portage Bay Rd. Turn left (east) onto Portage and drive about 6 miles to the campground.

Upper Peninsula

21 RIVERBANK SANCTUARY

For nearly 40 years, this relatively small Michigan Audubon Society preserve lay hidden away in the Upper Peninsula, unknown to even most of the organization's members. Though the society acquired the property in 1947, they didn't place signs there until 1986, the same year the local Audubon chapter discovered the sanctuary's existence. Today, the 23-acre parcel—which is surrounded by other natural attractions, including Indian Lake, magnificent Lake Michigan shoreline, and Palms Book State Park—remains a little-used gem of natural beauty.

The preserve, which lies along the south bank of the picturesque Indian River, shelters a startling array of Michigan flora and fauna, and the profusion of plant and animal life almost requires that you bring a small library of nature guides. The terrain alternates between low, wet bogs and sandy, wooded ridges. Tamarack, black spruce,

white cedar, yellow and paper birch, balsam fir, aspen, red and white pine, sugar maple and white oak create a many-shaded green canopy, with a wide variety of shrubs and ferns standing in the trees' shadows. Even closer to the ground, fragile mosses and delicate wildflowers add color to the landscape. Wild strawberries, Indian pipes, star flowers, Canada mayflowers, wild roses, Jack-in-the-pulpits, marsh marigolds, and forget-me-nots only hint at the profusion of seasonal blooms scattered within the preserve.

A host of wildlife also resides here or occasionally passes through, including three species of squirrels, snowshoe hares, skunks, beaver, deer and black bear. Common Loons, Bald Eagles, Pileated Woodpeckers, Wood Ducks, Ovenbirds and Evening Grosbeaks are only a few of the birds you might see.

County/City: Schoolcraft/Manistique

Fees: None.

Schedule: Open all year.

Directions: From the intersection of M-94 and County Rd. 440 on the northwest side of Manistique, drive approximately 1.5 miles west on CR-440.

Further Information: Michigan Audubon Society, 5011 W. St. Joseph, Suite 403, Lansing, MI 48908-0527.

22 BIG ISLAND LAKE WILDERNESS AREA

This rugged area in the Hiawatha National Forest is not for everyone. If you're willing to accept the challenge of making your own way through a near-trackless wilderness while living out of your backpack, or if you are a canoeist looking for an extensive system of lakes to explore or fish, then Big Island Lake Wilderness Area is a place you ought to visit. But if you just want a pleasant stroll along easily walked and well-established trails, turn to any of a hundred or so other pages in this book.

Although this area has felt and still exhibits the imprint of man's presence, it is wild, rugged and uncompromising. From county roads 437 on the south and 445 on the west, faint two-tracks penetrate the area, which is closed to motorized vehicles. But other than posted canoe portages that link many of the 23 small lakes in the region, there are no marked trails. A compass, a topographical map from the District Ranger Office (address, above right), and your orientation skills are all that's available to negotiate the land that's home to Pine Martins, bobcats, raccoons, porcupines, black bear, loons, beaver, ducks, Sandhill Cranes, and an occasional Bald Eagle.

The area was heavily lumbered between the 1890s and the 1930s, when first the pine and later the hardwoods were cut. Countless stumps stand in mute testimony to the lumberman's axe, and old logging roads, railroad grades and four abandoned logging camps add a ghostly eeriness to the area. In the hundred years since the lumberjacks' passing, maple, white birch, beech and quaking aspen have reclaimed the rolling hills, while hemlock, spruce and balsam inhabit the lowland areas and border the many streams and lakes.

You can backcountry camp throughout the wilderness area. Low-impact practices are encouraged, and you must carry out all refuse that you can't burn.

An average of 150 inches of snow fall here each winter, which makes for excellent opportunities for snowshoers and cross country skiers. As with hikers, only those with extensive outdoor experience should make solo trips.

County/City: Schoolcraft/Manistique

Fees: None.

Schedule: Open all year.

Directions: From Manistique, drive approximately 23 miles north on M-94 to County Rd. 437. Turn left (west) onto CR-437 and drive 2 miles to the wilderness area.

Further Information: Forest Supervisor, USDA Forest Service, P.O. Box 316, 2727 N. Lincoln Rd., Escanaba, MI 48929.

23 SCOTT'S POINT

Out of the way but not hard to get to, Scott's Point is the answer to a lazy man's wish for a deserted island. Even though you can drive right up to the beach on two-lane blacktop, when you take your first step out onto the almost untouched shore, it's not hard to imagine you've been marooned. Adding to the illusion is the sight of green humps of land 10 miles to the south. They're the Beaver Island Archipelago, and this the closest view of the islands across Lake Michigan from anywhere on either peninsula.

Anyone who loves to wade, play in the sand, sunbathe and beachcomb in splendid seclusion will find this the perfect spot for a day's outing. The wide, sandy beach ever so gently tips into the lake, and at some places the water is only ankle-deep 20 yards out from shore. In fact, the shoreline here is so tentative about where water should end and land begin, that sometimes the actual shore is indistinct. In some spots along the beach, the water covers the sand no deeper than coffee poured into a saucer to cool. It's a great area for wading, and the hardpacked beach is a sandcastle builder's dream come true.

Occasional areas of rocky cobblestone interrupt the flat expanse of sand. In places, wind and wave action has created long points of stone and bric-a-brac that reach well out into the shallows. You can walk 20 to 30 yards out into the lake on these miniature capes—the tops of which are barely three or four inches out of the water—and view the shoreline from a perspective that normally would involve getting at least your feet wet. Several swift-moving and icy-cold creeks cut channels through the beach on their way to Lake Michigan, and they not only add another touch of beauty to the surroundings, but also have a magnetic pull on kids of all ages who try to build Hoover Dams out of sand.

Back from the seemingly endless beach, inter-dunal ponds separate the sand from where the forest begins. The shallow ponds, shoreline and

forest attract and shelter a wide variety of wildlife, including terns, Piping Plovers and Great Blue Herons. Dwarf lake iris and Lake Huron tansy, two threatened Michigan plants, also find sanctuary here.

The only concession to humans at Scott's Point, other than the road leading to it, is a small picnic grounds set back from the beach in a sparse stand of cedar. The few tables are old and worn and the grills are rusty, which, all in all, seems more appropriate than if they were new and shiny.

(Photo, front cover.)

County/City: Mackinac/Gould City

Fees: None.

Schedule: Open all year.

Directions: From US-2 at Gould City, turn south onto Gould City Rd. and drive 9 miles to the park, at the road's end.

24 PRINISKI ROADSIDE PARK

On a 45-minute drive west from the Mackinac Bridge on US-2, so much beauty unfolds mile after mile that we almost begin to take it for granted and resist interrupting our journey to stop and soak in yet another fantastic view of Lake Michigan. The scenery at Rupert Priniski Roadside Park is, in truth, matched by several other spots along US-2, but there are a couple of good reasons to stop here. It is the last public stopping place on the lake for the next 50 miles west, and the area does hold a special significance. Within a mile west of the park, Lake Michigan reaches its northernmost point.

The park looks out onto a curving bay too small to frame the sweeping vista of Lake Michigan's sparkling blue water. A beach gently angles down to the water from the parking lot, and the light-brown sand extends in an arc to the headlands that mark the limits of the bay. Near the center of the park's shoreline, a jumble of rocks imbedded in the sand reach out from the land into the shallow Lake Michigan waters. When you're wandering along the shore or wading the surf, the line of natural stepping stones is irresistible.

From pine-shaded picnic tables and grills that border the parking lot, you get a scenic view few restaurants in Michigan can come close to matching.

County/City: Mackinac/Naubinway

Fees: None.

Schedule: Open all year.

Directions: Go 4 miles east of Naubinway on US-2.

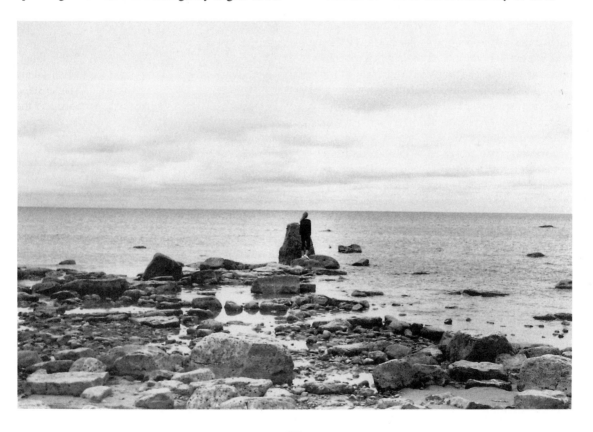

25 CUT RIVER BRIDGE

At 55 mph the view from the 641-foot-long Cut River Bridge is beautiful but brief. The cantilevered span, about four miles west of Brevort, carries US-2 over a deep gorge that the appropriately named river has chiseled from a high bluff overlooking Lake Michigan. The highway runs along the edge of the bluff, parallel to and about 100 yards back from the beach, and motorists crossing the bridge have a grandstand view of the lake 159 feet below.

You can get a longer and closer look at the scenery from two roadside parking lots, one at each end of the bridge, plus a trail that descends to the river. At the parking lot at the east end of the bridge, a picturesque, heavily shaded picnic area spreads over a thick, grassy lawn. From the picnic area, a paved footpath hugs the lip of the gorge as it passes just under the bridge's superstructure, then drops to the bottom of the bluff. The steep trail alternates between sharply inclined pavement, manmade stairs, and steps cut right into the hillside. Outstanding examples of mature white pine and red pine line the trail, and labels identify each species.

From the bottom of the bluff, it's only a few yards walk along the river to the lakeshore. The river cuts through pillow-soft sand on its last rush to Lake Michigan, and kids love to play civil engineer by trying to rechannel the water. From the bottom of the bluff, the trail turns inland and leads along the east bank of the river, passes under the bridge, and after about a 100 yards, climbs back up to the picnic area.

You can also take in the sights from the middle of the bridge on a pedestrian walkway that crosses the span. The view is thrilling, and so is the feeling of being less than a yard away, separated only by the width of a guardrail, from cars whizzing by at highway speeds. And if you get caught on the bridge when a semi-truck and trailer crosses, the swaying and vibration may be more memorable than the view.

County/City: Mackinac/Brevort

Fees: None.

Schedule: Open all year.

Directions: The bridge is approximately 4 miles west of Brevort on US-2.

26 SAND DUNES CROSS COUNTRY SKI TRAIL

This trail—a network of seven loops, which fit together like pieces of a jigsaw puzzle—is best known for its great cross country skiing on its regularly groomed tracks. But if you like to hike paths that are not compacted to the hardness of concrete by countless footfalls, you should set foot on this seldom-used complex of trails in the Hiawatha National Forest.

The hiking possibilities seem endless. Twenty hikers could start from the trailhead, which in the 1930s was the site of a Civilian Conservation Corps camp, and not follow the same route. Or better yet, one hiker could return 20 times and not follow his or her exact same footsteps.

The loops, ranging in length from 1.5 to 12.3 miles, wind through and across a series of old, wooded dunes. The trails pass under hushed hardwood forests thick with an understory of young trees and ferns, cut through a stand of red pines planted by the CCC in 1935, climb steep hills,

follow old two-tracks, and cross open country. The trail's light summer use is especially apparent where it knifes through knee-high weeds and grasses, with only a thin fold in the foliage showing where others have passed. For that reason and the constant company of mosquitoes, you should wear long pants. Blue trail markers plus maps posted at every trail intersection help keep you oriented.

County/City: Mackinac/St. Ignace

Fees: None for hiking, donations asked for skiing.

Schedule: Open all year.

Directions: From St. Ignace, drive 11 miles west on US-2 to Brevort Rd. Turn right (north) onto Brevort and drive 1/2 mile to the trailhead.

Further Information: St. Ignace Ranger District, Hiawatha National Forest, 1498 West US-2, St. Ignace, MI 49781.

Upper Peninsula

27 POINTE AUX CHENES

For 11 miles northwest of the Straits of Mackinac, US-2 and Lake Michigan flirt with motorists. The highway borders the northern reaches of Lake Michigan, and the great lake and its magnificent shoreline tease westbound traffic with peek-a-boo glimpses of stunning scenery. For brief stretches the highway runs alongside the beach, but before you can get your fill of the view, the road coyly strays inland or the lake hides behind tree lines or low dunes. When the highway cuts across the tip of Pointe Aux Chenes, about 10 miles west of the Straits, the lake is lost to view for over a mile as US-2 sets motorists up for a spectacular unveiling. The highway curves north along the west side of the stubby headland and then stretches out almost as straight as a guywire. For the next five glorious miles, US-2 borders one of the most beautiful and accessible beaches on Lake Michigan.

The blond ribbon of sand and limitless expanse of emerald-blue water compels even the hurried 55-mph traveler to stop, and there's plenty of room on the wide shoulder to safely pull off the highway. The wide, sandy beach begins at the very shoulder of the road and gently slopes down to the wave-lapped shore, where you can stake out a claim to a piece of sand as a base for beach-combing, sunbathing, and wading in the surf.

Across the road from the beach, low dunes rise toward the interior. Next to the road there, wildflowers and dune grasses sprinkle the sand, and stunted birches and evergreens cover the upper foreslopes of the dunes.

And there is more in this area than readily meets the eye. At about the halfway point on the five-mile beach, the Pointe Aux Chenes River flows into the big lake through a series of tortuous curves. On the inland side of the road, the river cuts through and drains the second-largest and least-disturbed marsh in the Great Lakes. This area, a small section of the Hiawatha National Forest, shelters more than two dozen rare and endangered species of flora and fauna in a wide range of habitats that includes at least 10 distinct biosystems. Lake Huron tansy, dwarf lake iris, pitchers thistle, Houghton's goldenrod, Bald Eagles, osprey, loons and terns all find refuge here.

County/City: Mackinac/St. Ignace
Fees: None.
Schedule: Open all year.
Directions: Drive 11 miles northwest from St. Ignace on US-2

28 HORSESHOE BAY WILDERNESS

Only minutes away from the hoopla and hype of the tourist attractions in Mackinaw City, St. Ignace and Mackinac Island is one of the best kept secrets of the Straits area. The Horseshoe Bay Wilderness Area lies within hailing distance of I-75 just six miles north of St. Ignace, but this section of the Hiawatha National Forest—with its seven miles of pristine Lake Huron beach and thousands of acres of swamp and forest—appears much as it did during the era of explorers and fur trappers. Though parts of the area were logged near the turn of the century, little evidence remains of the lumberjacks' efforts, and the land has been virtually untouched since their passing.

Inland, the area is marked by low, forested ridges and dense cedar swamps, where deer like to winter. While the forest and swamps are pretty, the lakeshore is stunning. From the edge of the tree line on the southern third of the seven miles of lake frontage, the soft, brown sand extends for as much as 50 yards before it dips into Lake Huron. Driftwood lies scattered, there are a few stretches of cobblestone, and except for a lone house visible far to the south on Rabbit Back Point, the beach is a limitless expanse of sand devoid of human intrusion. The northern two-thirds of the lakefront varies from marshy to rocky, and the entire beach is frequently backed by shallow interdunal ponds.

Access into the area is on the one-mile-long Horseshoe Bay Hiking Trail, which begins at the north end of Foley Creek National Forest Campground and breaks out of the woods onto the two-mile stretch of sandy beach. It's a long way to lug a cooler and beach chairs, but day-hikers can tote a small backpack and set off for a memorable day of exploring, beachcombing and playing in the surf. The easily walked trail crosses the cedar swamps on long strings of railroad ties and passes over low ridges, where young evergreens crowd the path. Moss and unusual ferns cover much of the ground, morel mushrooms peek out from the forest floor in spring, and if you look closely, you

might see insect-eating pitcher plants. Though the old trail has been well-worn by many years of use, you'll still usually see more deer tracks than human footprints.

The undisturbed wilderness also shelters bear, coyote, otter, mink, eagles, osprey, Great Blue Herons, gulls, shorebirds and numerous ducks.

The rustic (no flush toilets or electricity) Foley Creek Campground, on the southern edge of the wilderness tract, is one of the finest camping spots in the entire Straits area. All sites are heavily shaded, widely spaced, and screened by trees and shrubs.

County/City: Mackinac/St. Ignace

Fees: None for day use; $5 per night to camp at Foley Creek.

Schedule: Open all year. Camping at Foley Creek is on a first-come, first-served basis.

Directions: From I-75 approximately 6 miles north of the Mackinac Bridge, take exit 352 (M-123 exit) and go east about 100 yards to the Mackinac Trail. Turn right (south) onto Mackinac and drive approximately 2 miles to the Foley Creek Campground. The trail begins on the north end of the campground.

Further Information: Hiawatha National Forest, St. Ignace Ranger District, St. Ignace, MI 49781.

29 CARP RIVER

The 10,000-acre Carp River Wilderness Area (sometimes called the Mackinac Wilderness) is not for the faint-hearted or first-time outdoorsman. There are no marked trails into the area and no potable water. And don't even think about setting foot in the woods here unless you have excellent orientation skills, a compass and a topographical map. Depending on your enthusiasm, or lack of same, for exploring wild areas, Carp River is either that good or that bad.

Around the turn of the century, loggers stripped the area, and fires turned to cinder what little the lumberjacks left. But since then nature has reclaimed the land with a vengeance, and a dense 60- to 80-year-old second-growth forest now blankets a terrain of low sand ridges and wetlands. The Carp River, which dominates the wilderness here, flows in tight curves through the center of the tract, and numerous small trout streams lace the entire area.

Northern hardwoods dotted with stands of birch and aspen cover the generally higher ground of the parcel's north half. The south half is nearly impenetrable due to marshes and bogs. Several bea-

ver dams have flooded even more acreage.

Though inhospitable to man, animals thrive in the area. Osprey, Sandhill Cranes, Great Blue Herons, Pine Martins, Pileated Woodpeckers, mink, muskrats, Ruffed Grouse, raccoons, deer and black bear all reside here.

Except by canoeing the Carp River, the only way into the area is on foot over old roads, faint two-tracks and narrow trails. None of the routes are marked or posted, but some are shown on a topographical map available from the U.S. Forest Service in Escanaba for $1.00. The easiest access is via a trail that heads east from M-123 a half mile north of where the highway crosses the Carp River. This trail also allows the tenderfoot a taste of the wilderness, because for the first mile or so, the overgrown two-track is easy to follow and no other trails branch off. The track cuts through a dense forest with vegetation sometimes so thick you can't see 20 feet into the woods. Majestic clumps of white birch line the footway, and once away from the highway, the only sound you'll hear is your own passage through the forest. Other access points into the wilderness are widely scattered along forest roads 3450, 3119 and 3122, which border the area's south, east and north sides.

You can backcountry camp here, but you are asked to follow low-impact, no-trace practices. That means setting up at least 100 feet from any trail or water, preferably using a self-contained gas or sterno stove, and packing out all garbage that you can't burn.

County/City: Mackinac/Moran

Fees: None.

Schedule: Open all year.

Directions: Go approximately 12 miles north of St. Ignace on M-123.

Further Information: Forest Supervisor, Hiawatha National Forest, 2727 N. Lincoln Rd., Escanaba, MI 49829; (906) 786-4062.

30 PURPLE CONEFLOWER PLANT PRESERVE

On a seemingly insignificant clearing surrounded by the Hiawatha National Forest is one of Michigan's most puzzling botanical mysteries. North from Moran on highway M-123, the forest crowds both sides of the road for mile after mile. Then, on the site of the old ghost town of Kenneth, about halfway between Moran and Trout Lake, the forest draws back about 150 yards from the road for a half-mile stretch. The ghost town isn't a mystery. But the plant that blooms there late every summer—the purple coneflower—sure is.

By all rhyme and reason of nature, the purple coneflower should not survive in the inhospitable environment of the Upper Peninsula, some 25 miles north of the Mackinac Bridge. It is native to the Great Plains and thrives in Texas, Oklahoma, Kansas, and in a few spots in the dry grass plains of Illinois and Minnesota. Yet from late summer to first frost, this 21-acre clearing owned by the Michigan Nature Association is covered by a blanket of royal purple. The large, daisy-like blooms feature a deep-purple center, with swept-back rays or petals that vary in color intensity and hue from rosy brown to reddish purple. The flowers are at their peak of brilliance during the first two weeks of August. (Photo, back cover.)

A wide variety of other wildflowers and grasses dot the area, and the sanctuary is worth a stop any time of the year. In June, for instance, yellow lady's slippers put on an impressive display in the meadow that once held a town. Old foundations of a saloon and general store lurk at the northern end of the property. And rising from the flowers in the southwest corner, a rock the size of a car stands lonely vigil over the spot where the babies of Kenneth were buried.

No foot trails crease the meadow, and you are free to roam at will. But watch where you step, to cause as little harm as possible to both the plant life and yourself. Bedrock nudges out of the ground throughout the preserve where the thin layer of topsoil has eroded away. The low, flat expanse of rock shows the effects of centuries of erosion. Cracks and crevasses as large as a foot wide and four feet deep run through the stone, and you could easily twist an ankle with a wrong step.

The bedrock, only a couple of inches to a couple of feet under the topsoil, further compounds the coneflower mystery. On the prairie the flower sends a tap root seven to eight feet into the earth. Here that is impossible. How the flower got here and how it survives will probably forever remain a puzzle. (Photo, back cover.)

County/City: Mackinaw/Moran

Fees: None.

Schedule: Open all year.

Directions: From Moran, drive 7.5 miles north on M-123. The preserve is on the west side of the highway just south of the Kenneth Rd. intersection.

31 PINE BOWL PATHWAY

After passing rank after rank of perfectly aligned trees standing at woody attention, skiers or hikers at the Pine Bowl Pathway might begin to imagine they are reviewing the troops once stationed at Kinross Airforce Base, only two miles to the west.

The pathway's two loops, measuring 2.0 and 6.3 miles, cut in and out of an old pine plantation in the Lake Superior State Forest. The quiet, needle-soft trails also pass through a second-growth hardwood forest, and in the plantation you will occasionally see a lonely old hardwood with stones piled around its base, an indication that someone once tried to farm the area. The trails cross flat or gently rolling terrain and are wide, level and easily walked or skied. Maps of the pathway are posted at the trailhead.

County/City: Chippewa/Kinross

Fees: None for hiking. Donations are requested for trail grooming in winter.

Schedule: Open all year.

Directions: From I-75 16 miles south of Sault Ste. Marie, take exit 378 and drive 4 miles west on Tone Rd. to Wilson Rd. Turn right (south) onto Wilson and drive 3/4 mile to the trailhead.

Further Information: Area Forester, Sault Ste. Marie Forest Area, Box 798, 2001 Ashmun St., Sault Ste. Marie, MI 49783.

NORTHERN LOWER PENINSULA

32

40

39

41

42

45 44 43

46 47

48 38

55 49 50 51

54 53 52 37

56

57

33

34 35

36

Alpena

58 59

71 72

Traverse City

73

74

75

76

77

78 79

80

81 82

Grayling 68 69

70

68

67

60

62 61

63 64

65

66

32 BOIS BLANC ISLAND

As you clear Cheboygan Harbor aboard the small ferry, the low, green outline of the island that appears near the edge of the horizon seems to belie its name. French explorers called it Bois Blanc (white wood) for the great birch forest that ringed the island with its palisade of white trunks.

That birch forest, which blanketed the entire island, is long gone, but Bois Blanc remains an undeveloped natural wonderland that is overshadowed by the most famous island in the Great Lakes. While ferries crammed with sightseers depart every few minutes to and from Mackinac Island, the Plaunt Transportation ferry, *Kristen D*, at the height of the tourist season makes three trips a day to Bob-lo (as the natives call Bois Blanc), usually carrying only a dozen passengers and three or four cars. While Mackinac is crowned by the Grand Hotel and dotted with huge Victorian summer homes, Bois Blanc, except for a few small cottages, sits silent and green, appearing all but untouched by humans, even from only a mile off shore. In fact, the most striking view from the ferry as it crosses Lake Huron is not Bois Blanc but the Mackinac Bridge 15 miles to the north.

Once on the island, you may begin to think this might be the spot where the classic question, "If a tree fell in a forest and nobody was there to hear it fall, did it make a noise?" was first asked. A thick forest of spruce, fir, pine, beech, oak, maple and cedar covers the 23,000-acre isle. Sixty percent of the land is state-owned, and buildings occupy considerably less than 10 percent of the remaining property. The year-round population hovers at about 40 or so, with summer swelling the number to 1,000. The comforts of home and concessions to the tourist trade amount to a combination tavern/restaurant and a couple of cottages for rent. The one hotel on the island went out of business years ago.

In short, Bois Blanc is a quiet, lush, very special place to go to experience nature and the out-of-doors close at hand without anyone serving as an intermediary. You can beachcomb miles of deserted shoreline, find a secluded swimming beach, hope for a glimpse of a Bald Eagle or Osprey, and from the island's northwest tip, take in the most stunning view of Mackinac Island from anywhere in the Straits area. You can search for and identify 200 varieties of trees, flowers, and shrubs, including several of the state's threatened plant species that have found sanctuary here. Stands of old-growth red and white pine cover the center of the island, which has been undisturbed by settlement.

The 45 miles of roads that lace Bois Blanc vary from good gravel and soft sand to barely discernible two-tracks. They tunnel through dense forests, border Lake Huron for miles, and cut across the center of the island. They are seldom traveled by cars, however, which makes the island a great place for mountain bikers and backpackers. You can backcountry camp almost anywhere on state land, but you must get permission from the Cheboygan DNR office (address below).

County/City: Cheboygan/Cheboygan

Fees and Schedule: Contact the Cheboygan Chamber of Commerce (address and phone number below) for current ferry schedule and rates.

Directions: The ferry dock is in downtown Cheboygan, on Water St. just south of the bridge.

Further Information: Cheboygan Area Chamber of Commerce, P.O. Box 69, Cheboygan, MI 49721; (616) 627-2770. Or DNR Cheboygan Field Office, P.O. Box 117, Cheboygan MI 49721.

33 GORDON TURNER PARK

Gordon Turner Park proves that you are known by the company you keep. It's only 4.6 acres in size—most of which appears to be parking lot—and a large wetlands area makes its western boundary both indistinct and impassable.

But marking the park's eastern end is the busy Cheboygan River, and Lake Huron laps at its northern limits. From almost anywhere in the park you can see the Mackinac Bridge rising above the water 15 miles to the northwest. Directly north, 10 miles across the lake, Bois Blanc Island (see p. 34) cuts off the horizon. And the park, which is only three blocks from downtown Cheboygan, also provides a ringside seat to the busy little harbor, where pleasure boats constantly come and go and, less frequently, a ferry journeys back and forth to Bois Blanc Island.

You get the best view of the scenery and all the water-borne activity from a small picnic grounds laid out on a narrow strip of green between the parking lot and the lakeshore. East of the picnic tables and grills, a sandy swimming beach extends along the shore to a breakwater that marks the entrance to the Chebogyan River. The concrete pier reaches far out into the harbor and is a favorite spot of fishermen.

West of the picnic grounds, a boardwalk crosses a cattail marsh and ends at an observation deck overlooking a vast wetlands that borders Lake Huron. Open pools of water surrounded by acres of dense cattails and waving marsh grass attract numerous birds. With a pair of binoculars, patience and luck, it's possible to spot a wide variety of waterfowl and shorebirds without any exertion other than raising and lowering the glasses.

County/City: Cheboygan/Cheboygan

Fees: None.

Schedule: Open all year.

Directions: From US-23 about 3 blocks west of the river in downtown Cheboygan, turn north onto Huron St. Go 3 blocks on Huron to the park entrance.

34 PRESQUE ISLE COUNTY LIGHTHOUSE PARK

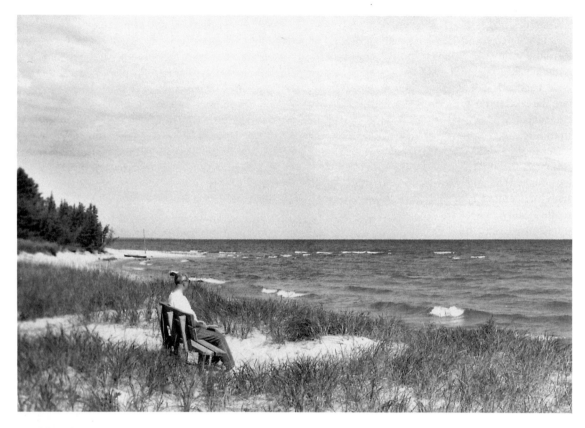

Although Huron ranks as the third-largest of the Great Lakes, in many people's minds it just doesn't have the same mystical or legendary fascination as lakes Michigan and Superior. If you're one who holds that view, stop at Presque Isle County Lighthouse Park and take in the limitless expanse of blue water that extends in a 180-degree arc to the horizon. No islands interrupt the immense sweep of water, and no headlands in either direction frame the view. You'll discover that lakes Superior and Michigan don't have a lock on size, beauty and mood.

A sandy, gently sloping beach—just right for wading, sand castle building, beachcombing and swimming—runs the length of the park. Forty Mile Point Lighthouse stands guard over this sec-

tion of the lake as a reminder that Huron can and does turn ugly and dangerous.

South of the lighthouse, which is not open to the public, a picnic area in a stand of birch and pine lines the back of the beach. Many tables and grills, although in full shade, are only a few steps away from the sun and sand. The light's foghorn building has been converted into a one-of-a-kind picnic pavilion.

County/City: Presque Isle/Rogers City

Fees: None.

Schedule: Open all year.

Directions: From Rogers City, drive 7 miles north on US-23.

35 SEAGULL POINT PARK

Curved like a scimitar, the three-quarter-mile-plus beach at Seagull Point Park is the main draw for most visitors. The Lake Huron coastline here *is* undeniably beautiful. The soft sand runs in a wide band along the shore before gently dipping into the lake and is reason enough for beachcombers, sunbathers and waders to make the short drive from Rogers City.

But there's more.

Behind the lightly used beach lies a series of low dunes that, although not as dramatic as the shoreline, entreat you to enjoy their fragile and subtle beauty. Spreading junipers, sand cherries, stunted pine and other shrubs creep down the foreslopes of the sandy hillocks and fight to retain a foothold on the easily eroded ground. On the inland side, small trees give way to larger ones.

A two-mile interpretive trail, which winds back and forth between the beach and the sparsley wooded dunes, crosses a small stream and is seldom out of sight of the lake. Interpretive signs along the route tell of the area's natural history and identify the flora. Crossing wide patches of soft sand slows the pace, and the trail takes at least an hour to walk, twice as long if you pause to enjoy the many striking views and investigate the complex and interesting dunal environment.

County/City: Presque Isle/Rogers City

Fees: None.

Schedule: Open all year.

Directions: From the intersection of US-23 and M-68 on the outskirts of Rogers City, drive north 1/2 mile on US-23 to Forest Ave. Turn right (east) on Forest and drive 1/2 mile to the end of the road. The parking lot and trailhead are on the left.

36 PRESQUE ISLE LIGHTHOUSE

𝑦 ⚒ ▌

There are two jewels in the crown of the Presque Isle Peninsula, and either one is worth driving out of your way to experience. A 90-acre park caps the very end of the strangely shaped peninsula—which, on a map, looks like a beckoning finger—and near the center of the park rises the tallest lighthouse on the Great Lakes.

The 109-foot-tall tower was put into service in 1870 as a replacement for an older, smaller light a mile to the south. (You'll pass it on your way to the top of the peninsula.) Set in front of the tall, white column is a carefully restored lightkeeper's house that, except for the cars parked outside, looks much as it did a hundred years ago. Inside, exhibits and displays relate the history of shipping and lighthouses on the Great Lakes, and one room furnished with artifacts and antiques looks so authentic that a lightkeeper from a hundred years ago could step inside and not feel out of place.

Several short nature trails, totaling more than a mile, begin at the lighthouse and circle the tip of the peninsula. Using a map that hangs in a small shed across the park drive from the lighthouse, you can choose walks from less than a quarter mile to any combination of routes up to 1.2 miles long. The trails border the rugged shoreline and weave in and out of evergreens and hardwoods. Trees along the way are labeled, and you can rest and enjoy views from strategically located benches. At the very tip of the peninsula, which is accessible either on foot or by car, a small picnic grounds and pavilion edges the rocky beach and looks out over Lake Huron.

County/City: Presque Isle/Rogers City

Fees: None.

Schedule: Open 8 a.m. to 10 p.m. all year.

Directions: From Alpena, drive approximately 10 miles north on US-23 to Grand Lake Rd. (Hwy. 405). Turn right (east) onto Grand Lake Rd. and follow it approximately 10 miles to the tip of the peninsula.

37 LOST TAMARACK PATHWAY

When you hike the Lost Tamarack Pathway, you don't have to worry about overcrowding or finding solitude. The trail system—two loops and one long point-to-point path that crease the secluded, rolling hills of southwestern Cheboygan County—is infrequently walked.

In the summer, access to the 4.75 miles of trails is from the beautifully wooded **Weber Lake State Forest Campground.** The quiet, secluded sites make a convenient and pleasant base camp for exploring this section of the Mackinac State Forest.

Loop One of the pathway heads north along the east shore of forest-ringed Weber Lake. The one-mile route curves around the north end of the lake, where it circles a spruce bog before backtracking to the campground. Loop Two breaks off from Loop One on the north side of the lake to inscribe a three-mile circle around both Weber and Little Weber lakes. The trail crosses several seasonal roads, passes through deep woods, and at its southernmost point, cuts through a hybrid aspen plantation.

If you'd like an even-longer hike, take a trail that leaves Loop One near its northernmost point and heads due north for 2.75 miles to where it joins the Wildwood Hills Pathway (see p. 40).

Because the dirt lane to the campground is not plowed in the winter, cross country skiers must access the ungroomed trails from a parking lot on County Road 58 two miles north from where Prue Road (which leads to the campground) intersects C-58. The winter trailhead is at the point where the connecting trail to Wildwood Hills Pathway crosses the county road. A map of the trail system and directions to the area are available from the address above, right.

County/City: Cheboygan/Wolverine

Fees: None.

Schedule: Open all year.

Directions: From Wolverine, drive 6 miles west on County Rd. 58.

Further Information: District Forest Manager, Mackinac State Forest, Box 667, 1732 W. M-32, Gaylord, MI 49735.

Northern Lower Peninsula

38   WILDWOOD HILLS PATHWAY

Wildwood Hills Pathway's three well-marked, easily followed trails take hikers and skiers into the heart of a northern Michigan second-growth forest. Ranging from four to over nine miles in length, three interconnected loops—stacked one on top of the other like a snowman—cross high, rolling hills in the Mackinac State Forest just a few miles south of Burt Lake.

From either of two trailheads on Wildwood Road, you plunge into a forest of hardwoods and evergreens marked by an understory of shrubs and ferns so dense that it's almost impossible to leave the trail in some places. The quiet woods give the sense of complete isolation, with the wind through the trees, an occasional bird call, and your own soft footfalls the only sounds you may hear.

Although long, the trails are easy walking, and you can bypass the few steep hills. Maps, which include mile markers, of the trail system are located at the trailheads and most major trail intersections.

The pathway is regularly groomed in the winter for cross country skiing.

County/City: Cheboygan/Indian River

Fees: None.

Schedule: Open all year.

Directions: From the intersection of M-68 and US-27 west of Indian River, go south on US-27 2 miles to Wildwood Rd. Turn right (west) onto Wildwood and drive 3 miles to the first trailhead or 4.5 miles to the second trailhead.

Further Information: Area Forester, Indian River Forest Area, Box 10, 6984 M-68, Indian River, MI 49749.

39 JOHNSON NATURE PRESERVE

Elmer Johnson Nature Preserve, owned by the Little Traverse Conservancy, is one of those rare private nature sanctuaries that you can enjoy either on foot or from your car. The preserve sits atop a line of high, heavily wooded hills almost a mile back from the Lake Michigan shoreline near Good Hart. From several clearings scattered throughout its 220 acres, you get spectacular, panoramic views of the great lake and the Beaver Island archipelago, strewn across the surface nearly 20 miles offshore.

A wide two-track ambles through open meadows and into the heart of a hardwood forest thick with giant maple and birch and scattered with boulders by the glacier that sculpted these hills. In the spring, wildflowers carpet the forest floor, and deer, fox and other wildlife are plentiful throughout the year.

Except for some moderately steep hills, the primitive road makes for easy walking and cross country skiing. Or if your vehicle has more than minimal ground clearance and you look carefully for fallen branches and avoid brush that may scratch paint jobs, you should also have no trouble driving the twin grooves.

County/City: Emmet/Good Hart

Fees: None.

Schedule: Open all year.

Directions: From M-119 in Good Hart, turn east onto Robinson Rd. and drive about one mile to Church Rd. Turn left (north) onto Church and drive 1/2 mile to the preserve, on the right-hand side of the road.

Further Information: Little Traverse Conservancy, 3264 Powell Rd., Harbor Springs, MI 49740; (616) 347-0991.

40 BEAVER ISLAND

✗ 📷 ⋀ 🚗 🏊 ⒣

At many places in Michigan, relaxation, seclusion and a chance to enjoy nature are options. On Beaver Island they're forced on you. This, the most remote inhabited island in the Great Lakes, is a detox center for compulsive workaholics and urban dwellers. Counted among the pleasures here is what you don't find—no McDonald's, no four-lane highways, no crowds, no fudge shops, no convenience stores and no pretense.

What you will find on this 13-mile-long, 3- to 5-mile-wide, 53-square-mile island includes almost unlimited stretches of deserted beaches, excellent backpacking opportunities, and beautiful scenery that includes deep woods, seascapes, seven inland lakes, small streams, cedar swamps, bogs, and abandoned homesteads and cleared fields left by early settlers.

The natural world here seems more sharply defined and intimate. That's not to say man's presence is not felt; the island is not a nature preserve. Yet rabbits overrun the land, it's unusual to take an evening drive without seeing numerous deer, and an active beaver colony thrives in the heart of the island. Coyotes, otter, fox and raccoon also roam freely, and 300 species of birds have been documented here over the years.

Two designated campgrounds plus the opportunity to pitch a tent anywhere on the state forest land that covers a third of the island add up to a perfect setting for some great backpacking. St. James Township Campground, on the north shore, is only a one-mile walk west from Beaver Island's lone town, St. James. The Jordan River State Forest Campground—on the east side of the island, adjacent to the largest tract of state land—is about seven miles south of the town's ferry dock. Camping at both is free and primitive, meaning no electricity or flush toilets.

The island is usually less than overrun by tourists, and for good reason. During most of the summer, only two ferries arrive daily, after a two-hour-plus voyage from Charlevoix. (The only other way to get to the island—unless you have your own yacht or airplane—is via McPhillips Flying Service from Charlevoix.) The total combined auto capacity for both ferries doesn't exceed 30 vehicles. Many visitors arrive without cars, either to backpack or just to leave another vestige of urban life behind.

If you don't bring your car and don't want to walk everywhere, Island Sports and Rentals leases cars, boats, bikes and mopeds. A taxi service is also available, and as a last resort, hitchhiking is acceptable.

Whatever method you choose, you can take hours or even days to fully explore the vaguely tear-drop-shaped island. One hundred miles of little-traveled, scenic roads lace the land, and many more miles of secluded, sometimes-faint foot trails lead into the most-remote corners. From the small village of St. James, at the north end of island, East Side Drive heads south and follows the sunrise shoreline past many of the island's summer homes on its way to the Jordan River State Forest Campground.

Across the road from the campground, a short trail system barely penetrates the approximately 15-square-mile main portion of state land that blankets the interior of the southern half of the island. This large tract of forest is the most inaccessible and undisturbed land on the island. A good gravel road circles it, some barely driveable trails cut across its western edge, and numerous faint trails head off into the woods and swamp from the boundary road. The trails border many beaver floodings, and if you're quiet, you may be lucky enough to see one, in addition to deer, fox, or even rarer, an otter or coyote. Berry pickers will find strawberries, blackberries, blueberries and cranberries.

East Side Drive continues south from the campground to Beaver Head Lighthouse and beautiful

Iron Ore Bay, on the island's south end. The Coast Guard abandoned the light in 1962, and it slowly fell into disrepair until 1979, when Charlevoix Public Schools personnel began restoring it for use as a summer education center. You can climb up an old spiral staircase to the top of the 50-foot tower for an unforgettable view of the nearby beaches and the Fox Islands, 15 miles to the south. Just west of the lighthouse, the road borders Iron Ore Bay. This sweeping arch of fine sand is one of the most beautiful and accessible beaches on the island.

Once past the bay, the road turns north and winds through deep woods as it heads up the west side of the island. Known there as West Side Drive, it rarely passes closer than a mile to Lake Michigan, but several dirt roads and less-passable two-tracks lead to within a half mile of the lake. From the end of any of them, a short walk will take you to miles of deserted surf-swept beaches. For a truly memorable day, pack a picnic lunch, grab a map, head to one of those many beach areas, and swim, beachcomb, sunbathe, and hunt for wildflowers or Petoskey Stones, all while out of sight of another human being.

The northern third of the island is webbed with roads that pass through more-open landscape. There, the haunting beauty of the fields, old orchards, abandoned farmhouses and decaying log cabins of the early settlers attract the lens of any passing camera.

An early evening trip to Bonner's Bluff, on the island's west shore, is a must. Natives and visitors both flock to the spot—easily reached by bicycle or car from St. James and then a short walk down a steep bluff that ridges the whole western side of island—to watch the sun set over Lake Michigan.

Virtually all the island's businesses and services are concentrated at St. James, which hugs the shore of picturesque Beaver Harbor. Two general stores attend to the basic needs of both vacationers and natives, and if you can't bear to cook, you have your choice of six restaurants. Several motels scattered around town provide clean, pleasant rooms. Also, housekeeping units and a wide variety of cottages and houses throughout the island are let on a weekly basis. You can get a complete accommodations list from the Beaver Island Civic Association (address below). And you can make any room reservation with almost certain assurance that upon arrival you will find neat, clean and comfortable quarters.

But—either as a reassurance or a warning—just because you take a room in town, you shouldn't jump to the conclusion that you will be at the center of what's happening (nothing is) or be bothered by the daily commerce of the island's capitol. In fact, it's just as easy to wile away the day undisturbed by cars, noise and busy goings-on in the center of this tranquil village as it is on some of the deserted beaches to the south. The high point of the day in town may be watching the ferry arrive or deciding whether to walk down to one of the two general stores to buy a Detroit paper. (That is, after a day or two, you even care about what's going on in the outside world.) And one more cautionary note. If you live to shop, you'll have a life expectancy of less than three hours.

Beaver Island's unique ambiance is matched by its unusual history. In the 1840s James Jesse Strang led a band of heretical Mormons to the island and, once there, announced to his faithful that he was Vice Regent of God on Earth. He made himself ruler of the Kingdom of St. James and turned Beaver Island into the only self-proclaimed kingdom in the United States. But Strang's reign was brief, and little remains of his rule except the Mormon Print Shop, which serves as the island's museum.

County/City: Charlevoix/St. James

Fees: Call the number listed below for current ferry schedules and fees. Cost for a vehicle and a family of four is about $100 per round trip.

Schedule: You can get to the island all year, but winter storms and bad weather can cut off ferry service.

Directions: Ferries to the island depart from a municipal parking lot next to the drawbridge in downtown Charlevoix.

Further Information: You can get ferry schedules and current costs, plus a list of accommodations from the Beaver Island Civic Association, P.O. Box 5, Beaver Island, St. James, MI 49782; (616) 448-2505.

Northern Lower Peninsula

41   M-119

Drive every other mile of blacktop in the Lower Peninsula and you still won't find a more beautiful or scenic 20 miles of Michigan highway south of Big Mac than the narrow, twisting ribbon of asphalt that connects Harbor Springs to Cross Village. The route, highway M-119, follows an old Indian trail and, with its several historical markers, is as rich in history as it is in scenery.

In the course of 200 years, countless moccasin-clad feet wore a narrow path along the edge of the high bluffs that guard this remote section of Lake Michigan coastline. Ottawa and Chippewa, on journeys to and from their villages in the vicinity of present-day Cross Village, stayed close to the edge of the bluffs, and M-119 follows the same path. While twisting through hairpin turns, the road tunnels through a magnificent forest of giant beech, sugar maple and eye-grabbing white birch. And for most of its length, the highway rarely strays more than a few feet from the edge of the towering headlands that rise from the lakeshore.

Just driving through the forest is memorable, but through numerous gaps in the wall of trees, you are also treated to some stunning views of Lake Michigan, the Beaver Island archipelago and Waugoshance Point. Spectacular at any time of the year, the drive is absolutely breathtaking at the peak of the color season, when a virtual caravan of cars and bicyclists stream up and down the highway.

Actually, the term "highway" is rather generous in describing this road. The 16-foot-wide snaking pavement is devoid of a centerline or shoulders. Huge trees stand within a foot or two of the roadbed, and for long stretches it is impossible to find room to pull off the blacktop. Drivers have to spend so much time watching the road, they have little chance to soak up the scenery.

County/City: Emmet/Harbor Springs

Fees: None.

Schedule: None.

Directions: Drive north out of Harbor Springs on M-119.

42 RAUNECKER NATURE PRESERVE

Though located within a few blocks of the swank, expensive and trendy gift shops of Harbor Springs and nearly surrounded by some of the most expensive resort property in northern Michigan, Raunecker Nature Preserve appears all but untouched by man.

No trails mark this 40-acre Little Traverse Conservancy preserve, but you can gain access from Fourth Street, which borders the tract's northern boundary. From there the land falls away to a low, wet cedar swamp. The hillside holds a stand of tall maples, and the lowland is studded with equally impressive cedars. In the heart of the preserve, downed trees, dense undergrowth, and wet ground in the lower reaches add up to rugged terrain and, at best, difficult walking. The sanctuary also features a pond, a creek and a naturally flowing well. The wild and untamed area shelters a wide variety of bird and animal life plus a pleasing number of wildflowers.

County/City: Emmet/Harbor Springs

Fees: None.

Schedule: Open all year.

Directions: In downtown Harbor Springs, drive west on Main St. to Traverse St. Turn right (north) onto Traverse and drive to Fourth St. Turn left (west) onto Fourth and drive approximately 1/4 mile to a city storage building, on the right-hand side of the street. Park there and enter the preserve by crossing the road.

Further Information: Little Traverse Conservancy, 3264 Powell Rd., Harbor Springs, MI 49740; (616) 347-0991.

43 BISSELL, (44) FISCHER and (45) JAMES NATURE PRESERVES

This trio of Little Traverse Conservancy nature preserves, just east of Harbor Springs, totals more than 55 acres of pristine natural beauty. Composed of upland woods, cedar swamps, a free-flowing well, a small stream, dense pines and evergreens, and downed, moss-covered trees, the preserves serve as reminders and examples of what the area must have looked like before Harbor Springs felt the presence of man.

Because the terrain of this small pocket of wilderness is so rugged, most visitors opt to view the area from Beach Road, a two-lane stretch of pavement that backs the three preserves. For the adventurous, a few access points and faint trails do allow close-at-hand exploration of the lush vegetation, bountiful wildflowers, and delicate ferns, plus a chance to seek out the numerous birds that inhabit the area.

The 3.5-acre pie-shaped S. A. Bissell Preserve is the westernmost of the three sanctuaries. On its east edge not more than 25 yards from the road, an artesian well springs from the ground and flows into a 55-year-old hand-built fieldstone reflecting pool. Adding to the charm of the setting, a tiny stream slips from the pool and winds its way to nearby Lake Michigan.

Also leading from the pool is a faint, seldom-trod footpath that, just a few steps directly east, crosses into the 50-acre C.A. Fischer Preserve's quiet world of lowland conifers and wetlands. The trail, however, is often wet, and walking can be difficult.

The smallest of the trio, the Dan and Ruby James Nature Preserve, lies across Beach Road from Bissell and Fischer. If the other preserves make for difficult walking, this two-plus acres of very wet cedar swamp is next to impossible to traverse, except on an old railroad bed that crosses the property. As with its larger counterparts across the road, James Preserve is rife with spring wildflowers and packed with untouched natural beauty.

County/City: Emmet/Harbor Springs

Fees: None.

Schedule: Open all year.

Directions: From the junction of US-31 and M-119, drive 2 miles north on M-119 to Beach Rd. Turn left (west) onto Beach and drive approximately 2.5 miles to the A.C. Fischer Preserve sign, on the north side of the road about 1/2 mile past Harbour Inn. Park on the roadside opposite the sign and either enter the preserves or carefully walk the road.

Further Information: Little Traverse Conservancy, 3264 Powell Rd., Harbor Springs, MI 49740; (616) 347-0991.

46 MEADOWGATE and (47) SANDFORD NATURE PRESERVES

These two adjoining Little Traverse Conservancy nature preserves are a study in contrasting ecosystems.

Just one-tenth of an acre shy of 10 acres, the Meadowgate Preserve is an old farm field that is slowly being reclaimed by nature. The Conservancy acquired the property in 1978, just as it appeared that a huge condominium complex would forever alter the landscape. But instead of buildings and asphalt, a colorful mosaic of tall grass dotted with staghorn sumac, apple trees, lilac bushes, and mature sugar maple covers the field. During the past 10 years, at least one bear and a Great Grey Owl have paid a visit. There are no trails, but you are free to traipse anywhere over the pleasant meadow.

Bordering the west edge of Meadowgate and standing in sharp contrast to it is Sandford Nature Preserve's one-acre parcel of picturesque hardwoods. Inside the dead-level tract, mature hemlock, beech and maple shoulder their way to the sky in competition for the sunlight. Below their thick canopy, the leaf-strewn forest floor stays in perpetual shadow during the summer. There are no trails, but there also is no dense understory. So walking is easy, and you will find the area carpeted with wildflowers in the spring and cool and secluded in the summer.

County/City: Emmet/Harbor Springs

Fees: None.

Schedule: Open all year.

Directions: From the junction of M-119 and US-31, drive 4.5 miles north then west on M-119 to Hedrick Rd. The preserves are on the south side of the highway, opposite where Hedrick Rd. meets M-119.

Further Information: Little Traverse Conservancy, 3264 Powell Rd., Harbor Springs, MI 49740; (616) 347-0991.

Northern Lower Peninsula

48   BAY VIEW WOODS

✻ ✦ ✽

Bay View, a picturesque community of Victorian summer homes and cottages that overlook Little Traverse Bay, deserves to be as famous for its nature preserve as for its unique collection of houses. Hidden away at the back of the labyrinth of winding roads that web the enchanting picture-book homes, Bay View Woods encompasses some of the most memorable natural beauty in the northern Lower Peninsula. The diverse habitat, cover and food attract plenty of birds, and bring your camera because the area almost begs to be photographed.

The beguiling mixture of scenery and ecosystems is easily accessible via four interpretive trails and several other paths that crisscross the area. A cedar/hemlock swamp, wooded ridges, lowland hardwoods, natural springs, wooded uplands, and steep bluffs that mark the former shoreline of a prehistoric lake give just a hint of the constant variety and beauty of Bay View Woods.

For an in-depth examination of the area, pick up a detailed, illustrated 16-page brochure and map at one of the preserve's two trailheads. The booklet—with numbered paragraphs that correspond to markers along the four interpretive trails—lists, for example, many varieties of ferns found here, including horsetail, ostrich, cinnamon, wood and regal. You can also use the brochure to search out numerous wildflowers, fungi, lichen and moss and help identify white and yellow birch, beech, hemlock, ash, sugar maple, striped maple, cedar, dogwood, wild cherry, balsam fir and basswood.

Easy access to the sanctuary comes from a small parking area at Richards and Knapp streets. From there the half-mile-long Old Indian Trail loops into the preserve and connects to all the other trails. Initially it follows the crest of a wooded ridge studded with imposing trees. When the trail leaves the ridge, it circles to the right and edges the bottom of a bluff, where numerous small springs trickle from the hillside, cross the path, and eventually become lost in a swamp bisected by the trail on its return to the trailhead.

Also on Knapp Street, two blocks west of the Old Indian trailhead, the Gateway Trail enters the sanctuary. This half-mile-long path circles through a stand of mixed hardwoods, many of which bear identifying labels, and also crosses a pretty stream that empties the swamp.

Another half-mile-long path, Deer Trail, connects the Gateway Trail and the Old Indian Trail, and you can only reach it by hiking one of the latter trails. While threading its way between the base of a bluff and low, swampy ground, Deer Trail meets several more rivulets that spring from the hillside and flow into the swamp.

The fourth interpretive route, a mile-plus unnamed trail, penetrates the far reaches of the preserve. Beginning at the south end of Gateway Trail, it climbs a steep bluff that used to form the shoreline of ancient Lake Algonquin, which covered much of the present-day Great Lakes and Michigan during the last ice age. While following the edge of the bluff and weaving through a wooded highland, you get a few glimpses of Little Traverse Bay plus a good look at the effects of the last ice age and erosion on the surrounding landscape.

If you don't get enough walking on the interpretive trails, you can take any of several other informal paths that wind through the preserve.

County/City: Emmet/Bay View

Fees: None.

Schedule: Open all year.

Directions: From US-31 in Bay View, make your way to the back of the community using Terrace and Forest avenues. From Forest Ave., turn onto Richards St. and drive to where it meets Knapp St. A small parking lot and the trailhead is at the corner.

Further Information: Bay View Association, Bay View, MI 49770.

49 COVERT WILDLIFE SANCTUARY

This 62-acre preserve—perched near the tip of a blunt peninsula that juts out into Walloon Lake—serves up a veritable smorgasbord of natural habitats. A dense pine plantation, open meadows and glens, hardwood-covered hills, berry patches, marshy wetlands, a secluded pond, and an abandoned orchard favored by deer, grouse and songbirds all grace this Little Traverse Conservancy wildlife sanctuary.

The land was donated to the Conservancy in 1980 with the stipulation that it remain in an entirely natural state. The lush diversity of untouched habitats attracts an abundance of wildlife, and the sanctuary has become a favorite of local nature photographers and birdwatchers.

No established or formal trails mar the landscape, and the Conservancy requests that visitors make only light use of the preserve.

County/City: Emmet/Petoskey

Fees: None.

Schedule: Open all year.

Directions: From the intersection of US-131 and US-31 in Petoskey, drive west on US-31 one mile to Resort Pike Rd. Turn left (south) onto Resort Pike and drive approximately 6 miles to where it deadends at Lake Grove Dr., at the small township park at the end of the road. Access to the preserve is across Lake Grove Rd. from the parking lot.

Further Information: Little Traverse Conservancy, 3264 Powell Rd., Harbor Springs, MI 49740; (616) 347-0991.

Northern Lower Peninsula

50   ORCHIS FEN

Orchis Fen is a naturalist's dream and a hiker's nightmare. The 38-acre fen—a low-lying land wholly or partially covered by water—harbors a number of striking plants. Sundew, bladderwort, pitcher plant and 19 varieties of orchids grow here. But this Little Traverse Conservancy preserve does not reveal its beauty or give up its secrets easily.

Plant life literally chokes the sanctuary. Moss and sedge cover the wet ground, and stands of tamarack, cedar and black spruce grow so thick that at times the preserve seems almost impenetrable.

Deer tracks score the soft ground everywhere you look, and game trails are also about the only routes for people into the riot of vegetation. Best

access comes from a small meadow on the northeast corner of the property. A compass, a good sense of direction, waterproof hiking boots, and plenty of insect repellent are necessities for exploring this area, which at best is difficult to walk.

Because of the fragile nature of the preserve, the Conservancy requests that visits be limited to individuals or very small groups.

County/City: Emmet/Petoskey

Fees: None.

Schedule: Open all year.

Directions: From the intersection of M-119 and US-31 north of Petoskey, take US-31 northeast about 200 yards to Pickerel Lake Rd. Turn right (east) onto Pickerel and drive 1.9 miles to Bellmar Rd. Turn left (north) onto Bellmar and drive 1/2 mile to the preserve, on the left-hand side of the road.

Further Information: Little Traverse Conservancy, 3264 Powell Rd., Harbor Springs, MI 49740; (616) 347-0991.

51 BEAR RIVER VALLEY RECREATION AREA

This 36-acre city-owned park traces a long, narrow ribbon of natural beauty through the center of Petoskey, yet hundreds of vacation-bound tourists pass over it daily without even knowing of its existence. In downtown Petoskey just before northbound US-31 bends left to follow the Lake Michigan coastline, the highway crosses an old concrete bridge. Below that bridge, hidden in a steep-sided valley cut by the Bear River, the park offers what many vacationers are searching for but are passing by—a chance to enjoy a picturesque outing in a natural setting.

The park follows the river valley for more than a mile back inland from the point where the Bear River joins Lake Michigan. In many spots, except for an occasional powerline and an infrequent glimpse of a house, you can almost imagine that you are in the wilderness. Once you're away from the bridge, the murmur of traffic is nearly drowned out by the rushing waters of the Bear River. The trail stays close to the banks of the river and passes mature birch, maple and white pine. Farther inland the trail climbs above the river to a waterfall created by an old power plant and its dam.

The open woods, areas of tall grass, dense thickets lining the river, shrub-studded hillsides and moving water attract numerous birds. Adding to the chances of good birding is the fact that the park is a natural oasis for wildlife in a busy and heavily populated urban area.

At the park entrance, on Lake Street directly across from City Hall, a small, pleasant picnic area edges the river just above a final dam before the river loses itself in Lake Michigan. In the fall you can be held spellbound at the sight of salmon trying to jump the dam as they attempt to swim upriver and spawn. The picnic grounds contains fewer than half a dozen tables and no grills, but there is plenty of room to spread a blanket and enjoy the surroundings.

In the winter cross country skiers find the park an easily accessible and beautiful area for enjoying their sport.

County/City: Emmet/Petoskey

Fees: None.

Schedule: Open all year.

Directions: From the junction of US-31 and US-131 on the south side of Petoskey, follow US-31 about 1/2 mile to Wachtel Ave. Turn left (north) onto Wachtel and drive one block to Lake St. Turn right (east) onto Lake and go 2 blocks to the park, directly across from city hall.

52   MCCUNE NATURE PRESERVE

Out of the way, strikingly beautiful, and lightly used yet easily accessible, this 168-acre Little Traverse Conservancy nature preserve has just the right mix of elements for a perfect outing in northern Michigan's wooded environment. And an added plus: You can match your outdoor experience to your skill and endurance.

From the parking lot just off a paved but little-used road, McCune's gently rolling and wooded terrain descends to the east branch of Minnehaha Creek, which cuts the sanctuary into two unequal sections. You can easily access the eastern parcel via a well-worn and comfortably walked nature trail. But exploring the west section requires the fording of at least one, and possibly both, of the creek's two branches and bushwhacking your own

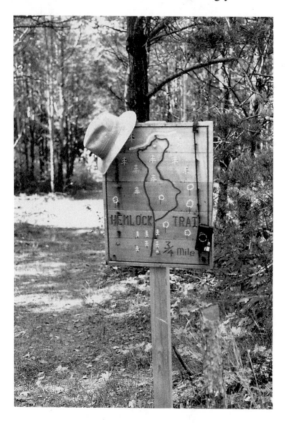

trail. You can walk the east side without fear of getting lost or wet, but if you want to head into the far reaches of the western section, a compass, a sense of direction and some basic outdoor skills are necessities.

The three-quarter-mile-long Hemlock Trail, on the preserve's east side, is a great introduction to the northern woods and will be a more-than-sufficient outdoor experience for most visitors. The trail, shaped like an old-fashioned rug beater, begins at the parking lot, next to a pine plantation. The first third of the trail, the handle of the beater, edges an open field then, just as it plunges into a forest of hardwoods, splits into a long oval that takes you to the banks of Minnehaha Creek.

After entering the forest, the trail makes a sharp four- or five-foot drop to the creek's flood plain, where the trees are so old and big that you are in perpetual shadow. You wind your way around some truly impressive hardwoods and evergreens before you meet the shallow, picturesque east branch of the stream. The fallen trees dipping into the stream, the dark and swiftly moving water, and the simmering reflection of the forest above is mesmerizing. After following the creek for a few dozen yards, the trail loops around to meet the handle and return you to the parking lot. The route also takes you past a variety of flora and through a great wildlife area where bear, beaver, deer, fox, rabbit, coyote, porcupine and numerous birds have either left signs or been spotted.

County/City: Emmet/Petoskey

Fees: None.

Schedule: Open all year.

Directions: From downtown Petoskey take Mitchell Rd. (Co. Rd. 58) east approximately 7 miles to Maxwell Rd. Turn right (south) onto Maxwell and drive 3/4 mile to the preserve, on the right (west) side of the road.

Further Information: Little Traverse Conservancy, 3264 Powell Rd., Harbor Springs, MI 49740; (616) 347-0991.

53 AVALANCHE PARK

Avalanche Park, on the south side of Boyne City, offers the most spectacular view of Lake Charlevoix and the surrounding countryside to be had from any vantage point in Charlevoix County. But there is a price to pay. Barn Mountain looms over and dominates the 320-acre city park, and there is no easy way up the steep slope to the observation deck on the summit.

For traditionalists a trail begins on the right-hand side of the huge hill and curves up and around its western face. Along this route you'll pass through a second-growth hardwood forest on a loose-sand trail that makes for some hard slogging. The forest is so thick that there's no view or visual perspective by which to judge how high you have climbed. You don't know how much farther it is to the top until you get there.

A more direct route leads straight up the open face of the mountain on a long series of staircases that total 460 steps. This route is also more monotonous, but at least when you stop for a breather and look over your shoulder, you get a view that broadens the higher you climb.

Either way takes stamina, but the magnificent view of Lake Charlevoix, the surrounding hills that seem to cup the lake, and Boyne City, which looks like an HO-scale modeler's layout, is worth the effort. And during the color season, nature takes a paint brush to the vast canvas to create an even more vibrant landscape.

If you have any energy left after the climb, you can walk trails that depart from the summit of Barn Mountain and circle through the surrounding high, rolling country.

In winter, locals and tourists flock to the park for downhill and cross country skiing or to zoom down the slopes on sleds and toboggans.

County/City: Charlevoix/Boyne City

Fees: None.

Schedule: Open all year.

Directions: From downtown Boyne City, drive south on Lake St. to its end. Turn left (east) onto Ann St. and follow it about a block to the park.

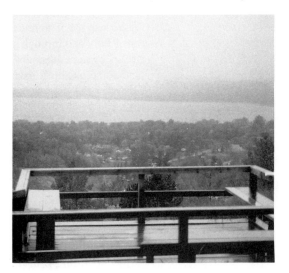

54   MT. MCSAUBA RECREATION AREA and
55   NORTH POINT PRESERVE

These two adjoining areas are prime examples of the unique and nearly indescribable beauty found only along the enchanted coastline of the Great Lakes. That this pair of natural wonderlands lie less than a mile from downtown Charlevoix, are easily accessible by car, and still have somehow escaped commercial development only adds to their special value as places to enjoy the gifts of nature. Together they total 79 acres of wooded dunes and more than a mile of gorgeous Lake Michigan shoreline.

North Point Preserve, the northernmost of the two parcels, is composed of 27 acres of low, wooded dunes and cedar swamps populated by world-class-size birch and cedar. The towering trees shade a thick understory of shrubby evergreens, vines that Tarzan would be proud to swing on, and a forest floor accented with wildflowers. A maze of trails meander every which-way through this other-worldly setting and give the impression that no matter how many times you visit, it would be impossible to duplicate an earlier walk. The dense cover, small clearings, and variety of plants, plus the nearness of open water suggest that the area could be excellent for birdwatching.

Fronting the maze of trails and deep, quiet woods is a rugged, rocky beach. The cobble, which extends for dozens of yards from tree line to find sassafras and mountain maple trees. The soft, sandy trails and steep climbs are tiring, but the scenery—including a glimpse of Lake Michigan from atop the piles of sand—and the sense of adventure in exploring the dunes' hidden nooks and crannies draw you up one slope after another. Not surprisingly, the area is also popular with skiers and sledders in the winter.

A walk to the beach reveals another side of the park. In contrast to North Point Preserve, the shoreline here resembles a monstrous sandbox. A wide strip of down-soft sand separates the tree line from the water, and you'll find the urge to walk barefoot along the edge of the surf nearly irresistible. The view is spectacular. South down the beach, the port of Charlevoix is clearly visible, while to the west and north, nothing but the blue-green waters of Lake Michigan reach out to the horizon.

County/City: Charlevoix/Charlevoix

Fees: None.

Schedule: Open all year.

Directions: Drive north, then east out of Charlevoix on US-31 approximately one mile to Mercer Rd. Turn left (north) onto Mercer and go one mile to Pleasant St. To reach North Point Preserve, turn left (west) onto Pleasant and drive 2 blocks to McSauba Rd. Turn right (north) onto McSauba and go 3 blocks to the parking lot.

To reach Mt. McSauba Recreation Area, turn left (west) onto Pleasant from Mercer and go one block to Pearl St. Turn left (south) onto Pearl and drive 1/2 mile to the parking area.

water line, is not for barefoot beachcombers. But tennis-shoe-clad explorers and photographers can search for waterfowl, pretty or unusual rocks, and water-sculpted driftwood. About 50 yards south—that is, left from the end of Mt. McSauba Road—you can get a commanding view of the point from a low observation platform nearly hidden in the tree line.

Just south of and sharing a property line with North Point Preserve is Mt. McSauba Recreation Area. Sawtooth-shaped dunes—indiscriminately interrupted by gullies, cuts and draws—characterize this 52-acre city park. A variety of unmarked but well-trod paths wind over and through tall dunes anchored against the wind by birch, beech and a smattering of pine and maple. If you like to search for the unusual, you can also

Northern Lower Peninsula

56   SPORTSMEN'S PARK

Sportsmen's Park cozies up to the south arm of Lake Charlevoix and the Jordan River at the point where the stream enters the long, narrow fiord-like lake. There's not much room to stretch your legs, but the postcard-size area will certainly give your eyes a workout. Only an Al Kaline throw away, at the opposite end of a bridge that carries M-32 traffic over the lake, is downtown East Jordan. From the small, grassy park and its half dozen picnic tables, you get a marvelous view of the quaint village, which hugs the lakeshore, and the low, wooded hills that ring the horizon and tumble down to the picturesque body of water.

The vista is beautiful, but most nature lovers will be drawn to scenery closer at hand. A sluggish creek and marshy area make an indistinct border between the park and Lake Charlevoix. And on the park's south end, the Jordan River separates the picnic grounds from a large natural area that surrounds the southern tip of the lake. The broad, slow-moving river, the great expanse of marshy wetlands, and the open water all attract rafts of waterfowl and numerous shorebirds.

With patience, a pair of binoculars or spotting scope, and virtually no exercise, you stand an excellent chance of seeing a wide variety of ducks plus geese, swans and marsh birds. And on a good day, binoculars aren't even necessary, as the birds paddle about near shore or wing by close over-

head. Many of the Canadian geese, Mallards and swans have become so used to visitors that they panhandle for food. Several Osprey nesting platforms in the area increase your chances of seeing that majestic bird.

County/City: Charlevoix/East Jordan

Fees: None.

Schedule: Open all year.

Directions: From the intersection of M-66 and M-32 on the west side of East Jordan, follow M-32 east into town approximately 3/4 of a mile to the park. The entrance is on the right, just before the bridge crosses Lake Charlevoix.

57 WARNER CREEK PATHWAY

Deer tracks often outnumber the heel marks of hikers on the soft ground of this lightly used trail, which takes both hikers and cross-county skiers through the picturesque Harwood Hills section of the Jordan River State Forest. The easily walked 3.8-mile-long single loop passes through stands of young pine and old maples and also skirts a swamp, the creek from which the trail takes its name, and at the halfway point, a large pond. Blue DNR trail markers lead from the parking lot on M-32 down a short access route to the main pathway, which circles through highlands overlooking the Jordan River Valley. Once away from the highway, you are enveloped in beauty and a quiet broken only by the call of birds or the rattle of wind through the trees.

County/City: Antrim/Boyne Falls

Fees: None.

Schedule: Open all year.

Directions: From the intersection of M-32 and US-131, go 1.5 miles west on M-32 to the parking lot, on the south side of the highway.

58 ASPEN PARK

Blindfold someone before taking them to Aspen Park, and they won't believe they are in a city park less than half a mile from a strip mall. The 100 acres of hilly, wooded and wild terrain seem more appropriate to the farther reaches of Otsego County rather than minutes away from downtown Gaylord.

The jumble of sharply rising hills is covered in a tangle of dense hardwoods, young white pine and low thickets. Deep depressions between the hills are wet with ponds and marshes. The broad assortment of habitats attracts numerous birds, and you'll have especially good chances of spotting warblers, upland game birds, and marsh and shorebirds.

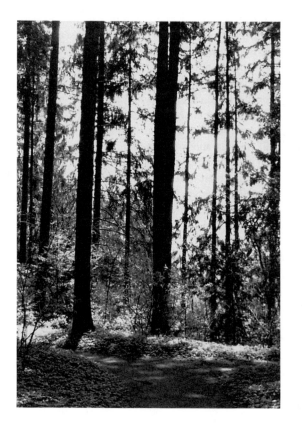

Two-tracks and trails lead every which-way through the park and appear to have evolved through random wanderings by visitors rather than by systematic design. Narrow trails descend into the water-filled depressions between the hills, with some of the paths so steep that on the way back up, you'll find yourself negotiating the paths on hands and knees while still remaining nearly upright. Other easier-walked routes circle the highlands, shoulder their way through dense woodlots, and occasionally allow glimpses of homes near the park.

The park also contains a picnic area and accommodates cross country skiers in the winter.

County/City: Otsego/Gaylord

Fees: None.

Schedule: Hours and days vary, but hikers and cross country skiers can always walk into the park from the gated entrance.

Directions: From downtown Gaylord, drive about one mile south on Business I-75 to Commerce Blvd., just south of the Kmart store. Turn left (east) onto Commerce and go less than 1/2 mile to Village Pkwy. Cross the intersection and enter the park.

59 BIG BEAR LAKE NATURE PATHWAY

The likely chance of spotting a beaver is the main attraction at this Mackinaw State Forest trail, but even without sighting North America's largest rodent, you'll leave with many pleasant memories.

The pathway's two loops total 2.2 miles and lead through a variety of landscape and habitats home to deer, porcupine, Ruffed Grouse, Woodcock, waterfowl and beaver. The shorter 0.8-mile Beaver Lodge Loop attracts the most attention because it circles a pond with an active beaver colony. The trail initially follows an abandoned railroad grade then edges a marsh-fringed pond and cuts through a stand of mature red pine. Once out of the pine, the trail circles the beaver pond and briefly follows the shoreline of Big Bear Lake before returning to the trailhead.

The longer Eagles Roost Trail carves a wide two-mile loop through country east of the Beaver Lodge Trail. During that approximately 40-minute walk, you'll thread your way through upland hardwoods, encounter a small pond and a dense stand of aspen, and pass through open areas carpeted with wildflowers. Occasional interpretive signs along both loops explain some of the natural and human history of this remote, out-of-the-way area.

Both trails begin and end at a large state forest campground that hugs the north shore of Big Bear Lake. An adjacent day-use area, including a picnic site, is a pleasant place to cool down after a hike.

County/City: Otsego/Gaylord

Fees: None.

Schedule: Open all year.

Directions: From Gaylord, drive 17 miles east on M-32 to County Rd. 495 (Meridian Line Rd.). Turn right (south) onto CR-495 and go 1.2 miles to Little Bear Lake Rd. Turn right (west) onto Little Bear and drive less than 1/4 mile.

60 JEWELL LAKE TRAIL

This lightly visited and out-of-the-way recreation area in the Huron National Forest certainly lives up to its name. You won't find any precious stones here, but the lake, campground, and especially the trail make up a gem of a spot for the quiet enjoyment of some positively serene natural beauty.

Jewell Lake, almost smack dab in the middle of Alcona County, is a crystal-clear pool in a sea of forest-green trees. The rustic national forest campground, on the south shore, contains 32 spacious sites that are well-shaded by a leafy canopy. A small, sandy beach and shallow swimming area are only a few steps away. Day-users will find a small two-table picnic area snuggled up to the lake at the boat launching ramp, east of the campground.

Capping off this delightful recreation area is the Jewell Lake Trail, which begins at the west side of the beach area. Only a few yards down the trail, a rustic footbridge spans a slow-moving stream edged by a picturesque cedar swamp. Across the bridge, the path makes a hard right and hugs the shoreline of Jewell Lake for almost half the trail's one-mile length. Cedar, birch and pine line the water's edge, while inland the forest floor is thick with ferns and an understory of young trees and shrubs. Eventually and almost regrettably, the trail turns inland and loops through a stand of birch and aspen before returning to the lake and the footbridge. Birds and wildflowers abound along the easy-walking path, which was constructed in 1974 by the Youth Conservation Corps. Two benches strategically placed along the route allow you to prolong your stay in this treasured corner of the national forest.

County/City: Alcona/Barton City

Fees: None for trail use. Camping fees are $5-$6 per night.

Schedule: Open all year.

Directions: On M-72 go either 14.5 miles west of Harrisville or 8 miles east of M-65 to Sanborn Rd. Turn north onto Sanborn and go 1.7 miles to Trask Lake Rd. Turn left (west) onto Trask and go 0.7 miles to Forest Service Rd. 4601.

61-64 RIVER ROAD NATIONAL FOREST SCENIC BYWAY

The River Road National Forest Scenic Byway is 22 miles of two-lane blacktop highway that you can drive in less than half an hour. But don't bet on it. The 4.3 miles of state highway M-65 and 17.7 miles of a county road known as River Road that together make up the byway pass some of the most spectacular scenery in the eastern Lower Peninsula.

The byway borders the south bank of the Au-Sable River atop highlands that rise 150 to 200 feet from the water. A series of four dams along this stretch of the historic trout stream create large impoundments, and a map of the AuSable looks more like either a series of long, narrow lakes or a single long serpentine body of water that has been corseted in four spots. The bordering highlands do not gently roll down to the river. Rather, the impoundments lap at the very edge of the sheer banks—or, more accurately, wooded cliffs—that rise up almost perpendicular to the water. When you stand at the lip of the banks, you get a breathtaking view of a water-filled valley dotted with marshy wetlands; flooded areas with old trunks protruding from the water; the steep, forested banks on the opposite shore; and, surprisingly, a towering sand dune nearly the equal of Sleeping Bear Dunes.

The catch at this scenic drive is that you can't appreciate or even observe most of the beauty and points of interest from your car. In fact, most of the byway is just a tunnel through lush, green forest. To truly enjoy this unusual and beautiful natural attraction necessitates exercise, some of it strenuous.

Four major facilities are strung out along the byway. To explore all four will take the better part of a day, yet each in its own right is worth a trip to the AuSable.

61 EAGLE RUN SKI AND NATURE TRAIL

Located two miles west of Oscoda on River Road across from Oscoda High School, Eagle Run holds 6.9 miles of the most-level cross country ski and hiking trails in the area. The broad paths burrow through the dense foliage of second-growth forest on the highlands that overlook the valley. Skiing and hiking are easy here, but this is also the least-scenic of the byway's five major attractions. The trails don't lead to the breathtaking views you'll find at the other spots, but you can enjoy a walk through the quiet solitude only a deep woods can offer. You can choose from three loops—which measure 1.0, 4.8 and 6.9 miles—and you can use a large map in the parking lot at the trailhead to help plan your outing.

(continued on p. 62)

Northern Lower Peninsula

RIVER ROAD NATIONAL FOREST
SCENIC BYWAY

(continued from p. 61)

62 LUMBERMAN'S MONUMENT

The largest tourist attraction and, arguably, the prettiest stop along the scenic byway is Lumberman's Monument, 15 miles west of Oscoda. The centerpiece here is a nine-foot-tall bronze statue that has become a landmark in Michigan. Composed of three figures—a sawyer with an axe and a saw, a river driver with a pivey, and a timber cruiser with a compass—the statue was completed in 1932 and dedicated as a tribute to the memory of Michigan lumbermen.

Surrounding the statue is a modest display of lumberjack memorabilia, a giant pile of logs tumbled as if in a game of pickup sticks, and exhibits

and displays that depict the lumbermen's work and lifestyle. A visitor center next to the monument is the focal point for a summer-long series of interpretive programs, which range from lumbering-era stories to presentations on Bald Eagles, Kirtland's Warblers, and the life of a forest firefighter. Books, stationery and other gift shop items are sold at the center.

A short walk from the statue takes you to the edge of a cliff that plummets in a near-vertical 160-foot dive to the AuSable River. The spot not only presents a stunning view of the valley but also is the stepping-off point for the most unusual interpretive nature trail in Michigan. The Stairway to Discovery, which descends 260 steps to the edge of the river, may be the only interpretive nature trail in the U.S. perched in its entirety on a staircase.

Signs at 10 stops along the way explain the area's unique natural history, and you can also pick up a printed guide at the visitor center. Hint: Plan to stop at the interpretive points on your way back *up* because, unless you're in incredibly good shape, you're going to have to stop for rests during the return trip anyway.

If you're not too tired from the stairway, or after a rest you can also take a 20-minute brisk walk down a footpath that begins to the right of the visitor center, edges the rim of the cliff, then climbs to the top of a towering sand dune and another impressive view of the surrounding landscape.

Lumberman's Monument is also a lovely setting for a leisurely picnic in the woods. Grills and picnic tables invitingly rest amid a stand of red pine near the parking lot. Next to the day-use area is a 19-site primitive campground.

Less than a mile west of the monument area, a turnout on River Road leads to another sweeping look at the valley. But unlike the rigors at Lumberman's Monument, you only have to take a few short steps before the valley opens up at your feet. In a tall pine on the near shore, look for an eagle's nest, which has been used continuously since 1985. Also, with patience and binoculars, on most days you can see our national symbol soaring over the impounded river.

63 IARGO SPRINGS

From a platform built out over the bluff edge at Iargo Springs, about two miles west of Lumberman's Monument, you get probably the most-panoramic view of the river from any spot on the byway. The river here has a slightly different character. Grass and sedge border much of the riverbank and soften the shoreline. And the AuSable gives no sense of moving or that it's even a river.

At the bottom of a long flight of stairs that starts at the overlook, Iargo Springs virtually pours out of the hillside. The creek's two forks seemingly materialize from the side of the hill, meet about 30 yards later, then flow only a short distance before joining the AuSable. It is a decidedly unusual sight, and the Chippewa Indians believed that the "magical" appearance of water held mystical and curative powers. Take your time fully exploring and investigating the picture-perfect setting, because the long climb back will leave you breathless from more than just the beauty.

64 ROLLWAYS

The last stop on the scenic byway is six miles west of Iargo Springs on state highway M-65. There, a small picnic area borders the bluff and overlooks the backed-up river. The tables and grills are scattered among shade trees only a few steps from the steep bank, which drops off to Loud Pond. And—yes—another flight of stairs makes its way down the bluff to the water's edge. Across Rollways Road from the picnic area, 19 pull-through camping sites are arranged in a loop along the bluff's edge.

County/City: Iosco/Oscoda

Fees: None for day use. Fee for camping.

Schedule: Open Memorial Day weekend through Labor Day.

Directions: A half mile north of where US-23 crosses the AuSable river in Oscoda, turn left onto Mill St., cross the river, bear right and follow Mill until it runs into River Road.

Further Information: Tawas Ranger District, P.O. Box 472, East Tawas, MI 48730.

Northern Lower Peninsula

65 TUTTLE MARSH WILDLIFE MANAGEMENT AREA

Tuttle Marsh is a Hyatt Regency for waterfowl. And for birdwatchers it's one of those rare areas where observing can be as productive from a car as on foot.

In spring 1990, as a result of a cooperative effort of the Michigan Department of Natural Resources and Ducks Unlimited, construction was completed of an earthen dam and water control system that created a shallow 380-acre impoundment and wetland in this small section of the Huron-Manistee National Forest. Previously, only shrubland, scattered areas of grass and sedge, and very little open water covered the area. To further increase nesting capacity, 35 earthen nesting islands were constructed, and future plans call for upland nesting enhancement.

Birding is good now, and as marsh vegetation colonizes the wetlands, it can only get better. The wetlands are expected to attract large numbers of migrating waterfowl, significant numbers of shorebirds and Sandhill Cranes, plus muskrats, mink, beaver and even Bald Eagles. Most important, an area that formerly produced an estimated 10 duck and only three goose broods annually is expected to yield 65 and 10, respectively. The species most likely to benefit from the impoundment are Mallard, Wood Duck, Blue-winged Teal, Canada Goose and the relatively scarce Black Duck.

All this potential for finding birds can come from the inside of your car or only a few steps from the roadside. Tuttle Marsh Road borders the impoundment area and, in fact, the earthen dam runs along the west shoulder of the gravel road for almost a mile. At many places the dam is just high enough to obscure views of the wetlands, but you only have to climb a few steps up the low dike to be able to sweep your binoculars across the broad expanse of water and marsh. An elevated observation platform is also scheduled for construction. On the east side of the road, marshy areas and small pools of quiet, grass-fringed water skirt the road.

County/City: Iosco/AuSable

Fees: None.

Schedule: Open all year.

Directions: From AuSable on AuSable Rd. (Old US-23), drive 5 miles west to Tuttle Marsh Rd. Turn left (south) and drive approximately 2 miles.

Further Information: Huron-Manistee National Forest, Tawas Ranger District, P.O. Box 472, East Tawas, MI 48730.

66 CORSAIR TRAIL SYSTEM

🚶 🚏 ⛷ ⛺

Situated in a lovely valley in the Huron-Manistee Forest, the Corsair Trail System bills itself as Michigan's Cross Country Ski Capital. And for good reason. More than 15 loops totaling 34 miles of well-marked trails make up this sprawling complex, and a map of the system looks like a web spun by a spider high on LSD. From the center, where the parking lot sits, loops and trails of varying lengths head out, connect with other trails, and eventually wind their erratic way back to the hub.

Groomed in winter, the trail complex is one of the longest and finest in the state for cross country skiing. And during the summer, both day-hikers and backpackers can wear down boot leather on the countless paths. It would take an Einstein to calculate all the possible trail combinations, but it's easy to plan a hike to suit your exact wishes, from a short walk alongside Silver Creek to a two-day trek around the entire system.

At the trailhead a large map of the system, etched on a tabletop-size board, will help you plan your adventure, and smaller maps with "you are here" markers are placed at all trail intersections. Trails in the valley floor border fast-moving creeks and streams. Others pass over rolling hills that in some places become chest pounders because of their steepness.

You can backwoods camp anywhere within the area, but you must set up at least 200 feet from lakes and streams and a minimum of 100 feet from trails. Day-hikers can stoke up before or ease hunger pains after their treks at a small picnic area at the trailhead.

This entire area was the hunting grounds of the Chippewa and Ottawa Indians until nature delivered a one-two punch. A great storm flattened the forest, and years later a forest fire turned the fallen timber to ash. As a result, the first white visitors considered the area a wasteland. The lush forest the trails wind through today are the result of reforestation by the Civilian Conservation Corps.

County/City: Iosco/East Tawas

Fees: None.

Schedule: Open all year.

Directions: From US-23 in downtown East Tawas, turn north onto Newman St. and drive 2 blocks to State St. Turn left (west) onto State and go about 1/2 mile to where the road bears right, onto Bridge St. Just after Bridge crosses the Tawas River, the road forks. Take the right-hand fork, Monument Rd. about 7 miles.

Further Information: Huron-Manistee National Forest, Tawas Ranger District, P.O. Box 472, East Tawas, MI 48730.

Northern Lower Peninsula

67 ISLAND LAKE RECREATION AREA

Framed on the north and south by the shores of Loon and Island lakes, Island Lake Recreation Area—with its rolling morainal hills, deep glacial potholes, and beautiful hardwood forest—is a quiet and beautiful alternative to the more heavily used state and county parks in the region. This unit of the Huron National Forest may be out of the way, little-known and relatively small, but it still offers a full compliment of outdoor activities.

A pleasant picnic grounds and small swimming beach at Loon Lake make up the day-use section. On the southern end of the area, a neat 17-site campground hugs the north shore of Island Lake. Each of the widely spaced sites has a paved slip, and a small swimming beach and picnic area are only a few steps away from any point in the rustic campground. The 65-acre lake supports good fishing for perch, bluegills, and large and smallmouth bass.

Connecting the two lakes and their facilities are two loops that make up the self-guiding Island Lake Nature Trail. The well-marked paths wander through a hilly, forested landscape carved by the glaciers of the last ice age. Twenty numbered stops along the route correspond to coded paragraphs in a brochure available at either the Mio Ranger Station or from a box at the campgrounds fee station. The brochure explains the natural history of the area and notes points of interest along the trail. From the trailhead at the campground, a round trip between the two lakes totals 1.2 miles on the short route or 1.6 miles on the larger loop.

County/City: Oscoda/Rose City

Fees: Day use is free. Camping costs $5-6, depending on the campsite.

Schedule: Open Memorial Day weekend to Labor Day.

Directions: From Rose City, drive 7 miles north on M-33 to County Rd. 486. Turn right (east) onto CR-486 and drive one mile.

Further Information: Huron National Forest, Mio Ranger District, Mio, MI 48647.

68 KIRTLAND'S WARBLER BREEDING GROUNDS

Kirtland's Warbler—a small bluish-gray bird sporting a yellow vest streaked with black—is Michigan's most unique inhabitant. The species wasn't discovered until 1851, and it took another 52 years to pinpoint that its only breeding grounds on earth were in northern lower Michigan. In 1903 Norman A. Wood found the world's first breeding pair in Oscoda County about a half mile from the Crawford County line and a mile north of the AuSable River. Every nest or breeding pair found since has been within 60 miles of the nest Wood discovered. But it's not like the tiny bird is overrunning the area. For the past 20 years, the *world* population of Kirtland's Warbler has averaged under 500.

The little bird's precarious hold on existence stems from its overspecialization. It will only set up housekeeping in jack pine stands that are from eight to 20 years old and usually more than 80 acres in size. Although it winters in the Bahamas, it will or can breed only under very specific conditions found in 12 Michigan counties.

Given the rarity of the bird, its unusual natural history, and the fact that its very existence as a species depends on managed jack pine plantations in Michigan, Kirtland's Warbler draws curiosity seekers and devoted birders from around the globe, all of whom want a glimpse of one of the world's rarest creatures.

But to ensure, as much as possible, the continued viability of the species, the U.S. Fish and Wildlife Service has closed the birds' nesting areas to public entry. You can only view them by taking guided tours conducted by the U.S. Fish and Wildlife Service from Grayling or the U.S. Forest Service from Mio. The free tours usually run twice a day, at 7 a.m. and 11 a.m., from mid-May through July 4. The exact days, dates and times may vary slightly from year to year, so write or phone for details before planning a trip. Late May and all of

Flint Public Library Photo File

June present the best chances for seeing the birds, and you should, of course, bring binoculars or spotting scope.

Kirtland's Warbler sightings can never be guaranteed, so a trip north for the sole purpose of viewing one can turn out to be a monumental goose chase. But if you *are* lucky enough to spot a bird, you'll join one of the most exclusive clubs in the world.

County/City: Oscoda/Mio and Crawford/Grayling
Fees: None.
Schedule: Write or phone for details.
Directions: Write or phone for details.
Further Information: U.S. Fish and Wildlife Service, c/o Michigan DNR Grayling Field Office, P.O. Box 507, Grayling, MI 49738; (517) 348-6371. Or U.S. Forest Service District Ranger Office, Huron National Forest, Mio, MI 48647; (517) 826-3253.

Northern Lower Peninsula

69 WAKELEY LAKE FOOT TRAVEL AREA

A picture-perfect lake undisturbed by any development is the focal point of this 1,415-acre natural area. Cupped in low, wooded hills and fringed by quiet marshes and whispering trees, Wakeley Lake is so pristine that loons nest here and eagles are a common sight.

The federal government purchased the area in 1986 to manage it as a sanctuary for wildlife, with emphasis on protecting the eagles and loons. To help preserve the natural setting, motorized traffic is not allowed, and the loon nesting area, on the north end of the lake, is closed to the public from March 1 through July 15.

The eagles and loons are enough to draw both serious and occasional birdwatchers, but this small corner of the Huron National Forest offers a lot more to birders. More than 100 species have been spotted here, including Wild Turkey, Great Horned Owl, Great Grey Owl, Red-eyed Vireo, Northern Goshawk, Yellow Rail, two species of grosbeak, numerous warblers, and the rare Northern Shrike. A bird checklist is posted next to a detailed trail map at the area's single entry point, on M-72.

From that lone trailhead, a wide, level, easily walked path cuts through an aromatic pine forest for a half mile, then breaks out of the trees at a small picnic area on the east side of Wakeley Lake. Beyond the open meadow and its pleasing view of the lake, a network of abandoned two-tracks and foot trails head off into the farther reaches of the preserve. The paths circle the lake, skirt swamps and marshes, and cross an upland forest of jack pine and oak in which young white pine are securing a toehold.

This is an ideal area for novice backpackers to test their stamina and skills. You can backcountry camp throughout the foot-traffic area, with two restrictions: You must set up camp at least 200 feet from the lake and, of course, can't camp in the loon nesting area during the restricted period.

You can fish from June 19 through August 31 but must release all catches for the benefit of the eagles and loons.

County/City: Crawford/Grayling

Fees: None.

Schedule: Open all year.

Directions: On M-72 drive approximately 10 miles east from Grayling.

Further Information: Huron National Forest, Mio Ranger District, Mio, MI 48647.

70 RED PINE NATURAL AREA

At one time, as DNR Area Forest Manager Don Torchia tells it, the Red Pine Natural Area "contained the (single) largest red pine in Michigan. But several years ago, a larger one was documented, and at the same time, the monarch red pine died. It is now the largest *dead* red pine in Michigan."

Though the old giant died—maybe even of chagrin after learning it was no longer the biggest of its species in the state—there are so many other pines of imposing size and magnificence that the area has been designated a National Natural Landmark. The old-growth stand of red pine and jack pine is even more impressive because the area has been undisturbed by man—and never will be. The DNR will intervene in the case of wildfire, but because the purpose of the preserve is to study the trees' natural changes, no other human influence is permitted.

A half-mile-long path that winds through the grove's flat terrain makes for a pleasant, even inspiring, walk. The scent of pine permeates the air, and old needles soften your footfalls on most of the hike. The majestic, old trees tower above the fern-covered forest floor, and you can spot them at every point on the compass, with some of the giants even crowding the trail. Interpretive signs scattered along the route explain the natural history of the forest.

County/City: Roscommon/Roscommon

Fees: None.

Schedule: Open all year.

Directions: On M-18 from Roscommon, drive north then east 6.5 miles to Silsby Rd. Turn right (south) onto Silsby and follow the signs to Kirtland College. From Kirtland College on Sunset Dr., go 1/2 mile east to the natural area parking lot, on the north side of the road.

Northern Lower Peninsula

71 PALMER-WILCOX-GATES PRESERVE

Mother Nature never seems to tire of creating magical beauty from wind, sand and water along Lake Michigan's seemingly endless shoreline. The jaded may, after the umpteenth breathtaking view, remain unmoved by yet another striking expanse of blinding-white sand framed by green-and brown-cloaked dunes on one side and emerald-blue water on the other. But even those most dulled by the constant beauty of Michigan's coastline can't help but pause and appreciate the setting of this Nature Conservancy preserve.

The long, narrow 15-acre preserve rests on the east shore of the east arm of Grand Traverse Bay. From anywhere on the beach, you have a memorable view of the picturesque bay and, four miles across the water, the equally beautiful Old Mission Peninsula, crowned by million-dollar homes, sprawling orchards and rolling hills.

From Bay Shore Road, which gives access to the preserve, low, wooded dunes hide the shoreline, but a short 30-yard walk from the road's shoulder reveals the glorious beach. The wide strip of sand gently slips toward the water from the low, sandy ridges anchored by hemlock, cedar, fir, pine, hardwoods and low-growing junipers. Hidden along the edges of the dunes and nestled in the woods are a bounty of rare wildflowers.

No trails, except the one leading to the beach, mar the fragile charm of the dunes, and visitors are urged to stay off the low, sandy ridges because even occasional foot traffic can threaten many of the plants' tenuous grip on life.

But the beach allows plenty of room for exploring. Beachcombers can build castles in the fine-grain sand or wade the surf that washes the pebble-strewn shore. Naturalists and birdwatchers will want to walk the shore close to the edge of the wooded dunes and search for the rare Lake Huron tansy and the many warblers that inhabit the area. Also be sure to keep an eye peeled for shorebirds and waterfowl.

County/City: Antrim/Elk Rapids

Fees: None.

Schedule: Open all year.

Directions: At the traffic signal on US-31 just north of the Elk River in Elk Rapids, turn west and drive 100 feet to Bay Shore Rd. Turn right (north) onto Bay Shore and drive 2 miles. Park on the shoulder of the road.

72 ELK RAPIDS COUNTY PARK

Elk Rapids County Park is as pretty a picnic spot as you can find on either arm of Grand Traverse Bay. Low, wooded dunes border a wide, sandy beach perfect for sunbathers, sand-castle architects, beachcombers and swimmers. You get pillow-soft sand, a gently shelving bottom, and a magnificent view of both the east arm of the long, narrow bay and the picturesque Old Mission Peninsula across the waters. And when children tire of wading, swimming and playing in the sand, they can make tracks to the playground equipment that edges the landward side of the beach.

Back from the beach, individual picnic tables and grills nestle in small openings in the dense evergreens, birch and hardwoods that cover the ridged dunes. Almost every picnic site offers seclusion and privacy. Some of the spots have a view of the beach through a screen of trees, while others are cut off from the shoreline by the low sand ridges and heavy woods.

A maze of sandy, paved and needle-strewn trails wind through the 13-acre park. The trails follow depressions between the interdunal ridges, cut through the dense woods, and continually climb and descend the closely spaced ridge lines. Even a short walk gives the pleasant illusion of traversing a much greater distance and, in spite of being in the middle of a picnic area, of walking through a quiet and little-visited woodland.

County/City: Antrim/Elk Rapids

Fees: None.

Schedule: Open Memorial Day to Labor Day.

Directions: From the traffic light on US-31 just north of the Elk River in Elk Rapids, drive 2 miles south on US-31 to South Bay Shore Dr. Turn right (west) onto Bay Shore and drive 1/2 mile.

73 POINT BETSIE DUNES PRESERVE

🚶 📷

After you've walked a quarter mile down the beach from a Nature Conservancy sign at the end of Point Betsie Road, you can almost convince yourself you have discovered a stretch of Lake Michigan shoreline all but untouched by man. True, the stroll does take you past a few homes (set well back from the beach) and the Point Betsie Lighthouse may still be visible over your shoulder. But the 71-acre Point Betsie Dunes Preserve, with its 1,100 feet of prime lake frontage, still appears primeval.

Lake Michigan rolls in on soft, white sand interrupted by bands of stones and pebbles that have been polished by the sand, wind and water. The beach gently rises 25 yards from the water line to low-lying dunes that begin marching inland.

The preserve's exposed position on the tip of Point Betsie makes life hard for the plants that try to colonize the area. Sand cherries and dune grass hug the front of the dunes and are the first to put down roots and stabilize the sand. Farther inland, stunted trees and shrubs claw at the sand. But the precariousness of their situation is evident by the numerous blowouts, areas where strong winds have undermined the plants and then blown bare the face of the dune. These are ideal spots to study plant succession.

Life may be harsh for the plant kingdom, but people and animals find it quite hospitable. Inland, the line of successively higher dunes cup interdunal ponds that shelter frogs, toads, turtles, other amphibians and shorebirds. The lakeshore invites waders and beachcombers to search for unusual stones and driftwood that has been sculpted by the elements then tossed ashore. And the commanding, panoramic view of the great lake can lure you into simply sitting and contemplating the sweeping sea of blue.

County/City: Benzie/Frankfort

Fees: None.

Schedule: Open all year.

Directions: From M-22 4 miles north of Frankfort, turn west onto Point Betsie Rd. Drive one mile to the end of the road, then walk south 1/4 mile to the preserve.

Further Information: The Nature Conservancy, Michigan Chapter, 2840 E. Grand River Ave., Suite 5, East Lansing, MI 48823; (517) 332-1741.

74 ARCADIA MARSH

Most northbound motorists who crest the hill that overlooks Arcadia Lake 16 miles north of Manistee on M-22 will dismiss the view as merely pleasant when compared with the more-stunning scenery just a few miles up the road at Sleeping Bear Dunes. But birdwatchers will instinctively ease off the accelerator as the car comes off the hill and approaches the shallow, marshy lake. They will immediately recognize the lake as a potentially great birdwatching area and one where birding can be productive from the roadside rather than after or during a long walk. If they stop, they will prove their instincts right. The Manistee County Audubon Society rates Arcadia Marsh one of the best birdwatching sites in their county.

M-22 crosses the lake on a long causeway, and only a short bridge near the middle actually spans the water. The wide shoulders on either side of the highway permit easy pulloffs at what is, in fact, the middle of the lake. From the rock-steady road-way, you have a panoramic view of the lake and the marshy fringe that rings most of its shore.

Be sure to bring binoculars and, for best results, also a spotting scope to search the lake for the numerous waterfowl and shorebirds that migrate through the area every spring and those that take up residence here during the summer months. Sandhill Cranes, teal, Buffleheads, swans, Marsh Hawks, Red-tail Hawks and eagles have all been sighted here in addition to a wide variety of songbirds.

Children, however, may find more interest in the turtles that line every log near the roadside or the carp that churn throughout the shallow water.

County/City: Manistee/Arcadia

Fees: None.

Schedule: None.

Directions: On M-22, drive one mile south of Arcadia or 16 miles north of Manistee.

Northern Lower Peninsula

75 WOODLAND MANAGEMENT TRAIL

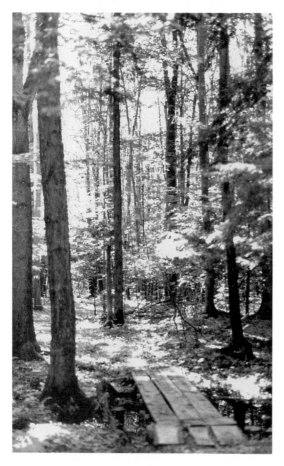

Whether you have a woodlot to manage or not, this easy walk through a beautiful natural setting is a fascinating educational experience. And when you do complete the three-quarter-mile-long trail, with its 22-page interpretive guide, you should merit an honorary diploma in woodlot management. The guide, compared to most interpretive brochures, looks like a textbook (study questions included). But don't be put off by its size; it's easy to use.

The guide's 19 numbered stops correspond to posts along the pathway, and at each you get a detailed but uncomplicated lesson on how forests can be managed for both wildlife and commercial interests. You learn, for instance, why aspen seedlings are important to deer and Ruffed Grouse, why Woodocks need open fields, how often pine plantations should be harvested, the significance of a wolf tree, the importance of woodlot ponds, and how to select hardwoods for thinning and harvesting. Using the booklet, you can also determine which trees are healthy and which benefit wildlife the most. You can get the guide in advance by writing the Manistee County Soil Conservation District (address below), or you can pick it up there during normal business hours.

Education aside, the trail presents a great opportunity to explore a beautiful and remote corner of the Manistee National Forest. The woodchip-covered path encounters a deep hardwood forest carpeted with ferns, a quiet pond, military-straight rows of red pines, open fields, an eerie swamp, and a slow-moving stream crossed by rough-hewn planks. Deer, raccoon, Wild Turkey, Woodcock, woodpeckers, squirrels and other wildlife inhabit the area.

County/City: Manistee/Bear Lake

Fees: None.

Schedule: Open all year.

Directions: From Bear Lake, drive 2.2 miles north on US-131 to Norconk Rd. Turn right (east) onto Norconk and drive one mile to the parking lot and trailhead.

Further Information: Manistee County Soil Conservation Dist., 6433 8 Mile Rd., Bear Lake, MI 49614.

76 TOWER PRESERVE

🚶 📷

A variety of dunal habitats, the glistening shore of Lake Michigan, and the absence of any concession to human use (except for several small property signs), make the 21-acre Lucia K. Tower Preserve a small gem of untouched beauty.

No trails mar the pristine beauty of this impressive Nature Conservancy preserve. A two-track briefly crosses the southeast corner of the property but quickly wanders off to the south. So if you want to experience the full flavor of the area, you need to take a compass and strike out on your own. Steep hills and the lack of well-trod paths require some strenuous walking, but you will be repaid with peace, solitude, and some unforgettable scenery.

The interior of the preserve holds a stand of large white cedar, several small swamps that darkly reflect the images of nearby trees, and hillsides covered with beech, birch and maple. In many places the overhead canopy so effectively blocks out the sun that you almost have to use a flash on your camera at noon, even in midsummer.

High dunes line the lakeshore, with Mt. Baldy, at 200 feet above Lake Michigan, presenting the most-breathtaking view of the wide expanse of watery blue that extends out to the horizon.

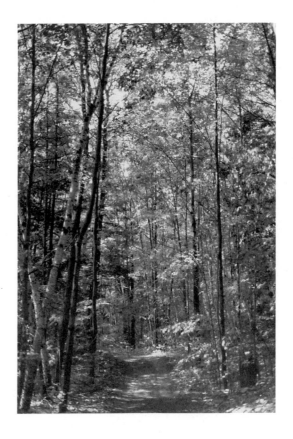

County/City: Manistee/Onekama

Fees: None.

Schedule: None.

Directions: From M-22 about one mile northwest of Onekama, turn west onto Portage Point Dr. and go 1.7 miles to Ivanhoe Rd. Turn right (north) onto Ivanhoe and drive 0.3 miles to just beyond where a two-track cuts off to the left. The preserve runs north and west from where the two-track intersects Ivanhoe.

Further Information: The Nature Conservancy, Michigan Chapter, 2840 E. Grand River Ave., Suite 5, East Lansing, MI 48823; (517) 332-1741.

77 LAKE BLUFF AUDUBON CENTER

One of the most unusual trees in Michigan grows at the Lake Bluff Audubon Center, on Lake Michigan. Relatively speaking it's still a baby, even at more than 60 feet tall and four feet in girth at its base. Its size, however, isn't what makes it particularly unusual, because it's a member of one of the longest-lived and largest species on earth—Sequoia redwoods. A Sequoia redwood? In Michigan!?

Lake Bluff began in 1936 as the private estate of M.E. and Gertrude E. Grey, and they spent years developing their acreage into a beautiful combination of natural landscaping and a carefully planned arboretum. In 1949 they brought several species of redwood seedlings to Lake Bluff in a single one-pound coffee can. Three, including the large Sequoia, survived their cross-country transplanting and continue to grow to maturity in our state.

But these "Baby Hueys" of the plant kingdom aren't the only outstanding natural attraction at the 70-acre estate, including a third of a mile of Lake Michigan shoreline, that was donated to the Michigan Audubon Society in December 1987 upon the death of Mrs. Grey. More than 150 varieties of shrubs and trees surround the estate house and grace the well-kept grounds, which run to the edge of a bluff that rises above Lake Michigan. Telephone-pole-size Douglas firs, white spruce, alder, huge old cottonwoods, black locust, white ash, weeping beech, red maple, Chinese juniper, spindle tree, Norway spruce, gingko, English holly and many others join the redwoods.

All shrubs and trees are labeled, and most are close enough together that you can take in a continent's worth of species in a very short walk. Adding to the enjoyment of a stroll through this unusual and magnificent collection are views of Lake Michigan, which come from almost everywhere within the arboretum.

Open meadows and woodlots make up the acreage away from the estate house. A large, open meadow studded with Bluebird boxes edges the southern boundary of the estate's formal lawn, and across M-110 a 40-acre woodlot holds a dense stand of second-growth maple, beech, hemlock, birch and oak.

The sanctuary's location on the Lake Michigan Flyway, the wide variety of flora, and the good cover all attract a great many birds. During spring and fall migrations, waterfowl and accipiter movement can be heavy.

Future use at this newest (as of 1992) Audubon nature center is in the planning stages, but most assuredly, opportunities for enjoying Lake Bluff will improve each year.

County/City: Manistee/Manistee

Fees: None.

Schedule: Open all year.

Directions: From the junction of US-31 and M-110, drive 2 miles north on M-110 (Lakeshore Dr.) to the estate, which is not marked by a sign, at 2890 Lakeshore. Park either on the shoulder of the road or in a one-car parking area in front of a farm gate about 20 yards south of the estate driveway.

Further Information: Manistee County Audubon Society, 5374 Orchard Hwy., Manistee, MI 49660.

78 MAGOON CREEK NATURAL AREA

This 97-acre tract of land overlooking Lake Michigan from atop a wooded bluff has felt the soft tread of moccasin-clad Indians who camped here each summer, the hobnail boots of lumberjacks who felled white pine that once grew here, and the iron-shod hooves of plow horses that worked the land at the turn of the century. But humans haven't touched the area for the past 50 years, and today, people are only occasional visitors to the dense woods and meadows that are slowly being returned to nature.

Magoon Creek offers so many options, that it induces "cross training" in outdoor enthusiasts. Picnickers won't be able to resist the nature trail or the beach. Hikers will have trouble maintaining an even pace as they pass interpretive signs, and beachcombers will find the woods and meadows as compelling as the lakeshore.

A one-mile self-guided nature/hiking trail winds throughout the preserve, including the picnic area and beach. Forty-four stops along the route make learning tree and shrub identification easy. At each stop a plaque identifies an important tree, shrub or fern in the immediate area—paper birch, red oak, red maple, juniper, Norway spruce, black willow, white oak, tamarack, poison ivy, white pine, beech, blackberries, horse chestnuts and wild grapes, to name a few—then explains both its natural history and importance to people and wildlife. You can also pick up an interpretive brochure, which has the same information as the plaques, from the Manistee Area Chamber of Commerce, on US-31 just south of the bridge over the Manistee River.

The trail pierces some prime wildlife habitat, where fox and deer are plentiful, and also passes through an area that contains the largest concentration of Bluebirds in Manistee County. The local Audubon chapter also rates Magoon Creek as an excellent birdwatching spot for warblers, upland birds, woodland species and birds of prey.

A small, secluded picnic area, accessible either by the trail or by road, is set in a dense stand of second-growth trees at the very edge of the bluff. The canopy of trees completely shades the area, and with the cooling effect of Lake Michigan at your very feet, you'll rarely feel the full brunt of Michigan's midsummer heat.

From a parking lot a quarter of a mile south of the picnic area, a several-hundred-yard downhill tramp ends at a little-used stretch of sand and surf. If you plan to spend a day on the beach there, pare what you want to take down to the bare essentials, because you'll have to haul it all back uphill to your car.

County/City: Manistee/Manistee

Fees: None.

Schedule: Open dawn to dusk all year.

Directions: From Manistee, drive approximately 4 miles south on US-31 to Fox Farm Rd. Turn right (west) onto Fox and go 3 miles to Red Apple Rd. Turn right (north) onto Red Apple and go 1/2 mile.

79 BIG MANISTEE RIVER STATE GAME AREA

This is one of the hottest birding spots in their county, says the Manistee County Audubon Society. Wood Ducks, warblers, owls, terns, wrens, and a surprising variety of other shorebirds and waterfowl all pay visits to this state game area, through which the last six miles of the Manistee River flows before emptying into Manistee Lake. State highway M-55 cuts through the heart of the area, and you have excellent chances of spotting birds just by pulling off to the side of the pavement and sweeping the wetlands with a pair of binoculars. Spring and fall visits will result in the most sightings, but any time of the year can be rewarding.

The game area is kept flooded to create a wetland habitat, and the dikes that help control water level provide ready-made walkways. From just south of the bridge that carries M-55 over the river, one broad dike forms a large half moon of dry land between grassy wetlands and the swift-moving Manistee River. That easily walked dike makes a fine vantage point for searching the marshy area that, in addition to birds, also shelters numerous fur-bearing animals. A canal that hugs the dike for several hundred yards harbors frogs, turtles, and small birds, which hide in the vegetation that crowds the lily-pad-dotted ditch.

A three-quarter-mile walk down the half-moon dike takes you to an observation platform built by the Manistee Audubon Society. The tower rises about 15 feet above the dike and offers a sweeping view of the wetlands to the west and the tree-lined Manistee River to the east.

County/City: Manistee/Manistee

Fees: None.

Schedule: Open all year.

Directions: From the junction of M-55 and US-31, drive 1/2 mile south on M-55. Park along the shoulder anywhere south of where M-55 crosses the Manistee River. A one-car parking area at the dike with the observation tower is 200 yards south of the river on the west side of the highway.

80 COOLEY BRIDGE

The stockade of trees that lines both sides of M-55 from Cadillac to Manistee opens up temporarily about 25 miles east of Manistee as the highway crosses a deep river valley. The view is both unexpected and pleasing. Steep walls frame the lush valley, and a broad ribbon of water traces the floor of what, by Michigan standards, could be called a canyon. But the traveler who takes in this view at 55 miles per hour misses an opportunity to experience even more outstanding beauty, both man-made and natural.

From a car Cooley Bridge looks like little more than two lanes of blacktop stretched across the green chasm. But from underneath or even from the side it becomes readily apparent why the American Steel Institute named this bridge the most beautiful in the nation costing less than a quarter of a million dollars. The graceful steel arch is beautiful for its geometric lines, functional simplicity and the way it fits into the landscape. Rather than bridging the valley, the curving steel seems to keep the two near-vertical walls from slamming together and erasing the work of thousands of years of flowing water.

On the east side of the bridge, a quiet grass-covered picnic area hides in a grove of evergreens. The tables and grills are set up only a few feet from a drive that circles through the trees and are back too far from the valley walls to provide any stunning views. But at the west end of the grounds, you can get some great views of the picturesque valley and the steel artistry from a long wood staircase that descends to the river.

County/City: Manistee/Wellston
Fees: None.
Schedule: Open all year.
Directions: On M-55, drive 2 miles west of Wellston or 25 miles east of Manistee.

Northern Lower Peninsula

81 SHEEP RANCH PATHWAY

🚶 ⛷ ⛺

It's not often that we're blessed by somebody else's financial ruin, but that's the case for hikers who walk the Sheep Ranch Pathway. As in most of northern Michigan, the area through which this trail passes was heavily lumbered in the late 1800s. But the lumber company that felled the white pine here went bust before they could level all the trees. As a result, you can enjoy a few imposing specimens of Michigan's state tree while walking the trail.

There's plenty of other memorable scenery along the pathway's two loops through this corner of the Pere Marquette State Forest. The trails cross several small streams, edge swamps, climb low hills, and traverse several pine plantations and stands of jack pine and oak.

The one-mile-long Lake Loop connects Big Leverentz and Little Leverentz lakes and the state forest campgrounds nestled next to them. Ten sites make up the campground at the larger lake, and at the south end of the loop, you'll find seven sites at Little Leverentz Lake. Neither lake, with their muddy bottoms, is suitable for swimming, but fishermen will find perch, bluefish, pike and bass awaiting their bait.

The pathway's River Loop swings in a 2.3-mile arc to the north of the smaller Lake Loop. At the farthest point, just before the trail turns back south, you reach an overlook with picturesque views of the Baldwin River, the first river in the state in which German brown trout were released.

In winter the pathway expands to 4.5 miles of ungroomed cross country ski trails.

County/City: Lake/Baldwin

Fees: None for hikers. There is a small charge for overnight camping.

Schedule: Open all year.

Directions: From Baldwin, drive 2 miles east on US-10.

82 GREEN PINE LAKE PATHWAY

Experienced hikers and greenhorn backpackers alike have several options to choose from at this trail system that cuts through the Au Sable State Forest. The Pathway—which totals 11 miles and includes three loops, measuring 1.0, 2.5 and 5 miles—connects Pike Lake State Forest Campground on the east to Mud Lake State Forest campground, on the west. You can plan hikes that range from short, pleasant walks to a two-day roundtrip with overnight stays at the campgrounds.

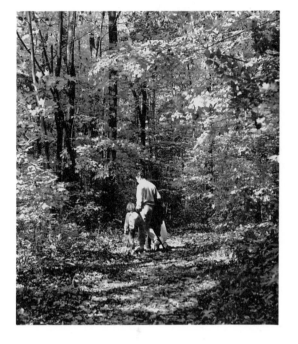

On the Pathway's eastern side, a 5-mile loop circles a large swamp. Stacked on top of that large loop on its north side at Green Pine Lake is a smaller 2.5-mile loop, and perched at its "top," its northernmost point, is the 30-site Pike Lake State Forest Campground. On the system's extreme west edge, a single one-mile trail loops east from the small eight-site Mud Lake State Forest Campground. A 2.5-mile trail that links the small loops at either end of the Pathway curves around numerous bogs filled with delicate and unusual flora ranging from tamarack trees to carnivorous plants and exquisite orchids.

Although both campgrounds cozy up to lakes, neither offers good swimming. But fishermen might like to take a break from hiking to go after bluegills, perch, bass and pike in both lakes.

County/City: Clare/Farwell

Fees: None for trail use.

Schedule: None.

Directions: From the junction of US-10 and M-115, go 7 miles north on M-115 to the Pike Lake Campground.

Northern Lower Peninsula

SOUTHWESTERN
LOWER PENINSULA

84
85

86
87
88 89

83

Muskegon

90   91

96

92

Grand Rapids

101

103

102

Kalamazoo

100

96
97

98 99

95
93 94

The focal point of this 591-acre park is the beautiful, clear and swift-moving Chippewa River which, like a piece of discarded ribbon, twists and turns for three miles through the heavily wooded landscape. Other draws to this flagship of the Isabella County park system include two suspension footbridges that connect to a scenic and extensive trail system, a covered bridge open only to foot traffic, several picturesque picnic areas, an interpretive nature trail, good fishing, a swimming beach, rustic and uncrowded campgrounds, and groomed cross country ski trails.

Two swaybacked suspension footbridges mark the north and south trailheads to the park's seven-mile-plus network of wide, well-marked footpaths, and crossing either of the spans is the only way onto the system. Three named routes pass through the gently rolling, wooded terrain on the east side of the river. The River Loop Trail sticks close to the Chippewa, and you'll catch several glimpses of the hurrying water from atop the high banks. That loop also crosses a covered bridge, from which you can usually see fish hovering in the crystal-clear water. The Wildwood Pathway takes a more direct route, over hillier and more-remote landscape, between the two cable-hung bridges. Several small cutoffs run between the Wildwood and River loops, which allows you to choose jaunts of varying lengths and scenery. At the north end of the park, walking the half-mile-long Oak Ridge Interpretive Trail—with 10 numbered stops keyed to descriptions in a pamphlet available at the trailhead—is a good way to learn about the surrounding forest.

A sandy swimming beach is cupped in the backwaters of the river, and the park is loaded with choice picnic areas. Along the main entrance road, you can stake claims to tables at three different areas: at the beach, well back from the river in the Elm Branch Picnic Area, or in the shadow of the north suspension bridge. For a mini-adventure you can lug picnic basket and blankets across the span and spread out on the shore of the Chippewa where it broadens into a large pool before sweeping under the bridge. An even more out-of-the-way picnic spot borders the river at the south entrance of the park off Winn Road.

A small, primitive campground (no flush toilets or showers) covers part of the north bank of the river only a short walk from either the swimming beach or the north trailhead bridge. A backcountry campground, accessible only by canoeing the river or hiking the River Loop Trail, sits on the east bank about halfway between the two trailheads. Its remoteness ensures a degree of privacy not usually found in downstate campgrounds, and it's also a good testing ground for backpackers who are planning more ambitious trips into the wilds of northern Michigan.

County/City: Isabella/Mt. Pleasant

Fees: $3.00 daily vehicle permit, $15.00 annual permit. Half price for senior citizens.

Schedule: Open 8 a.m. to 10 p.m. all year.

Directions: The main entrance is 5.5 miles west of Mt. Pleasant on M-20. To reach the south entrance, drive 1/2 mile west of the main entrance on M-20 to Winn Rd. Turn left (south) onto Winn and go 3 miles.

Further Information: Isabella County Parks Dept., 200 N. Main St., Mt. Pleasant, MI 48858; (517) 772-0911.

This 1,000-acre expanse of marsh and wet meadow rates as a pretty undistinguished stretch of landscape. But people don't drive out of their way—and the wetlands *are* out of the way from practically any place in the state—for the scenery. They come to see the unusual visitors that return here spring through fall, year after year.

America's third-largest bird, the Sandhill Crane, favors the area as a courting grounds, nesting site, and staging area for fall migrations. Cattle graze part of the refuge, which is part of the old Walkinshaw farm, now run by Merle Lass. Lass also manages the area for the Forest Service to support the cranes, and the birds evidently like the accommodations. Their numbers have steadily grown over the years, and Lass says he has noticed a marked increase in breeding pairs in the 13 years he's been at the farm.

The cranes arrive in mid-March and stay through mid-October. During nesting season, in early summer, the 40-inch-tall birds with seven-foot wing spans can be rather secretive, but in spring and fall they put on a spectacular show. In the spring young birds try to attract a mate for life through a dance that involves strutting, bowing, jumping, and even stick tossing, all of which is accompanied by a great deal of cackling. And in the early fall, more than 200 cranes gather here, like a giant tour group preparing to go south for a winter vacation.

You can observe the birds from the road that borders the wetlands, and you're also welcome at the farm. Sightings are never guaranteed, but the best time for ensuring a successful visit falls between late September and early October. And for best results then, as in spring and summer, arrive early in the morning or late afternoon.

You can spot other birds in the wetlands, too, such as Marshhawks, American Bitterns and White Egrets.

Flint Public Library Photo File

County/City: Oceana/Hesperia

Fees: None.

Schedule: Mid-march to mid-October.

Directions: From Hesperia, drive 2 miles west on M-20 to 192nd St. Turn right (north) onto 192nd and drive 6 miles to where the road bends sharply right (east). Follow the bend and drive approximately 1/2 mile to 198th St. Turn left (north) onto 198th and drive 2 miles to the wetlands, which start just north of the intersection of Fox Rd.

85 PINES POINT RECREATION AREA

The picturesque White River and the dense lushness of the Manistee National Forest create a quiet, pastoral mood at this little-used national recreation area.

A day-use area lies tight against the north bank of the rust-colored river. The apparently little-used picnic grounds there are wedged into a narrow isthmus that barely keeps a long loop of the river from forming a complete circle. Picnic tables are scattered under a tent of pines and hardwoods on a low bank that overlooks the river. Tubers and canoeists love the spot, because they can launch their craft on the north side of the picnic grounds, drift for half an hour with the current, then land on the south end of the picnic area only a few yards on land from where they started.

From the back of the picnic area, the seldom-trod, one-mile-long Pines Point Trail cuts a lazy oval through the forest. Except for areas where the route crosses a mature pine plantation or follows an old two-track, ferns and low-growing plants crowd the path so tightly they will brush your legs. At times, in fact, the trail appears to be only a crease in the green carpet that covers the forest floor, but it is well marked and easily walked over the rolling terrain.

Not far from the day-use area, several widely spaced and well shaded campsites—many with excellent privacy—rest on a low bluff that overlooks the White River.

County/City: Oceana/Hesperia

Fees: $1.50 day-use fee.

Schedule: Open all year.

Directions: From Hesperia, drive 2 miles west on M-20 to 192nd St. Turn left (south) onto 192nd and go one mile to Garfield Rd. Turn right (west) onto Garfield, go 3 miles, then follow the signs to the recreation area.

Southwestern Lower Peninsula

86　LODA LAKE WILDFLOWER SANCTUARY

This 1,000-acre haven for native Michigan plants is both a treat for the senses and highly educational. A one-mile-long trail, with 39 numbered interpretive posts, wanders through a collective microcosm of Michigan habitats—including a small lake, a bog, marshes, meadows and forests—filled with an astounding number of both common and endangered native plants.

The Federated Garden Club of Michigan, in cooperation with the U.S. Forest Service, began development of the sanctuary in 1938. Native Michigan plants were transplanted into the preserve, and those already there were nurtured and identified. But don't come expecting to see an arboretum, flower gardens or even informal plantings. The preserve is wild with flowers, shrubs and trees scattered across the landscape in a completely natural setting. The only concessions to people are a small picnic area at the trailhead, a boardwalk that crosses a wide marsh, the one-mile trail that partly follows an old two-track, and the numbered posts and a few benches along the path.

Be sure to draw your eyes away from the sweep of Loda Lake or the dense forest and take a close look at the delicate beauty underfoot. A brochure, available at the trailhead and the U.S. Forest Ranger Station on M-37 in White Cloud (chances are better for getting it there than at the trailhead), will help you identify ferns, violets, swamp rose, wild orchids, carnivorous plants, trillium, and many other delicate, beautiful species. Numbers in the pamphlet correspond to the numbered posts.

As you would expect in an area of such rich and diverse habitats, birds find the sanctuary to their liking. Waterfowl call at the lake, shorebirds and marsh birds nest and feed in the wetlands, and songbirds flit among the trees. If you pick up the interpretive brochure, you won't need to bring a wildflower guide, but until such time as birds can be enduced to sit on numbered posts, be sure to bring binoculars and a bird book.

County/City: Newaygo/White Cloud

Fees: None.

Schedule: Open all year.

Directions: From White Cloud, drive 6 miles north on M-37 to Five Mile Rd. Turn left (west) onto Five Mile and drive one mile to Felch Ave. Turn right (north) onto Felch and go one mile to the entrance, on the right-hand side of the road.

87 MANISTEE TRAIL

🚶 ⛺

The crossing of several roads and one Michigan highway keeps this 30-mile pathway from being a 100 percent wilderness experience. But because of the beautiful scenery along the other 99.99 percent of the route, hikers and backpackers usually voice no complaints. And in one way, the trail/road intersections are a plus, because they provide a choice of access and stopping points that allow you to tailor an outing to your liking.

The trail, which runs generally north and south through the Manistee National Forest and the heart of Newaygo County, creases high, rolling country dotted with fields, pine forests, large stands of mixed hardwoods with a sometimes-dense understory of ferns, and large openings in the forest created by clear-cut lumbering. Foot-

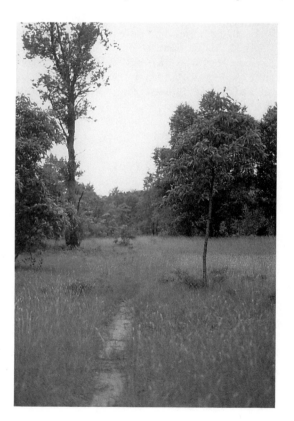

bridges and even logs carry hikers over numerous streams that cut across the trail. Deer are plentiful, and it's rare if you don't see or at least hear them moving through the forest.

Three rustic campgrounds are all located along the southern third of the route. You can also backcountry camp anywhere along the pathway as long as you set up at least 200 feet off the trail and 200 feet from lakes or streams.

You don't have to walk the entire trail, which starts at 40th Street about five miles north of Newaygo. You can also step onto it at Pierce Drive, M-20 and other east-west roads. For a complete trail guide and map that marks all access points, write to the address below.

Parts or all of the Manistee Trail will eventually be incorporated into what will be the longest hiking route in the U.S., the North Country Trail, which will run from Maine to North Dakota.

County/City: Newago/White Cloud

Fees: None.

Schedule: Open all year.

Directions: From White Cloud, drive one mile north on M-37 to M-20. Turn left (west) onto M-20 and go 2.7 miles to the trailhead. Or, from White Cloud go south 5 miles on M-37 to 40th St. Turn right (west) and go 3/4 mile to the trailhead. For other access points, write for a map at the address below.

Further Information: Michigan Trailfinders Club, 737 Billantau, S.E., Grand Rapids, MI 49508.

Southwestern Lower Peninsula

For nature lovers the YWCA's Camp Newaygo boardwalk beats Atlantic City's hands-down. The one-mile wood trail treats you to some truly unusual scenery while taking you across a huge marsh and bog and into the heart of a fascinating environment. The dead-level, easily walked boardwalk, which is wide enough for wheelchairs, is elevated just inches above a riot of vegetation sprouting from "land" that perpetually has the consistency of a water-laden sponge.

Delicate, vibrant and colorful wildflowers grow within inches of the boardwalk, and the lacey leaves of giant ferns crowd its edges. Unusual and fascinating plants seem to be everywhere, and when you lift your eyes from the wonders at your feet, you are assailed by the striking beauty of the cumulative effect of the low-growing jungle of plant life.

From several places where the trail widens, you get views usually only available from a boat or after a long, wet wade through dense vegetation. One of the observation platforms overlooks a bog that has reduced a lake to a small, dark pond ringed by sphagnum moss. The still, reflective waters ringed by green looks like a setting out of a fantasy where someone comes to cast a spell. From benches at another platform, you can relax and enjoy a panoramic view of the marsh and a grove of dead trees drowned by the wetlands.

The area is as rich in wildlife as it is in plant life. Woodpeckers hammer at dead trees; Great Blue Herons, Kingfishers and other birds hunt the shallow waters for fish; you can see turtles sunning themselves; and you might even spot a muskrat or raccoon slipping through the water or grass.

County/City: Newaygo/Newaygo

Fees: None.

Schedule: Open dawn til dusk, April through November.

Directions: From Newaygo, drive 4 miles north on M-37 to 40th St. Turn left (west) and drive 2 miles to where the road makes a sharp left (south) at a golf course and becomes Gordon Ave. Follow Gordon about a mile to 48th St. Turn left (east) onto 48th and drive 1.5 miles to the entrance.

Prairies are one of the rarest ecosystems in Michigan. Only an estimated 0.3% of the state's total land mass, or about 100,000 acres, was originally prairie. And with the coming of European settlers, it quickly disappeared under the plow because farmers didn't have to clear trees to start planting crops. But in many cases, the prairie soil was sandy, dry and ill-suited for cash crops, and farmers abandoned it.

Such was the case at the Newaygo Prairie Plant Preserve, now owned by the Michigan Nature Association. The land was last worked in the late 1800s, and since then prairie plants have slowly reclaimed the area. Today this 110-acre preserve reveals one of the few remaining large expanses of dry prairie in the state, and it's a strange sight for those of us used to seeing a landscape filled with trees, vast lakes or wetlands.

The main portion of the sanctuary fills a shallow tree-fringed bowl with a wide assortment of grasses and sun-loving wildflowers. The more than 100 plant species that populate the preserve put on a colorful show from early spring through late fall. In spring the prairie is covered with delicate wildflowers that hug the earth. As summer

arrives, taller plants and grasses reach maturity. By late summer and early fall, the heavyweights put on a spectacular display, with eight-foot-tall big bluestem, Indian grass, goldenrod and sunflowers dominating the plain.

Poplar Avenue borders the west side of the preserve, so even from your car you can appreciate the prairie's unique features. But you should take at least a few steps into the entirely different environment of strange grasses, plants and flowers. You don't have to bring a plant identification guide to enjoy the area, but it will certainly make for a much richer experience.

County/City: Newaygo/Newaygo

Fees: None.

Schedule: Open all year.

Directions: In Newaygo from M-37 just north of the Muskegon River, turn east onto Croton Dr. and go approximately 2.5 miles to Poplar Ave. Turn left (north) onto Poplar and drive 1/4 mile to the preserve, on the east side of the road.

Further Information: Michigan Nature Association, Box 102, Avoca, MI 48006.

"Hold it right there!" you're probably thinking. "What in the name of all that's holy to nature lovers is a sewage treatment plant doing in a book on natural attractions?" Well, the fact is, this is one of the state's great birdwatching areas, a place where year after year you can, with little effort, observe a staggering number of birds rare to Michigan.

Each spring the broad, flat, sandy plains that surround the treatment facility are planted with cash crops. The recycled wastewater from the plant, which is collected in two 800-acre diked lagoons, is used to irrigate the farmland. The extensive fields, shallow lagoons, dikes, and small woodlots at the fields' edges draw an enormous number and variety of birds, especially shorebirds and waterfowl. And, almost as though they were made for birders, one-lane roads follow the top of the dikes to make spotting easy.

Baird's Sandpiper, Buff-breasted Sandpiper, Stilt Sandpiper, Willet, American Avocet and Red Phalaropes are just some of the unusual and rare shorebirds you might spot along the edges of the lagoons. In late September through October, thousands of ducks and geese congregate on the holding ponds. Western Grebes and Eared Grebes call each spring and fall, as do such rare to Michigan gulls as the Glaucous, Iceland, Thayer's and Little.

Vultures and birds of prey, including Gyrfalcons and Peregrine Falcons, have been spotted in the area, and in spring the small woodlots attract good numbers of songbirds.

Yellow-headed Blackbirds, Wilson's Phalaropes, Upland Sandpipers, Bobolinks, Grasshopper Sparrows and Eastern Bluebirds are just a partial list of other interesting birds you will most likely see while slowly driving atop the narrow dikes. This is not only a great area for avid birdwatchers, but also an ideal location for novice birders to get hooked on America's fastest-growing sport. Need-

less to say, it would be a crime to arrive here without binoculars and bird identification books. Peak season for birding runs from mid-July until the ponds freeze over.

County/City: Muskegon/Muskegon

Fees: Daily passes onto the dikes are free and are available at the headquarters building, near the plant's entrance. Audubon Society members can obtain a yearly pass by showing their membership cards.

Schedule: Open 8 a.m. to 5 p.m., Monday through Friday.

Directions: From I-96 9 miles southeast of Muskegon, take exit 10 (Nunica exit). Go north 9 miles on 112th Ave.—marked B-31 on state highway maps and which becomes Maple Island Rd.—to a blacktop road that junctions from the east. (You will first cross M-46 and Hall Rd.) This is the entrance road; turn right (east) and drive to the headquarters building.

Though relatively small, this 128-acre nature preserve takes in a remarkable range of scenery and habitat—upland forests, open fields, a swamp, a marsh, a bog, a creek, a pond, a lake, a pine plantation, a wildflower garden and an arboretum— and they're all easily accessible.

Eight well-marked trails, totaling six miles and ranging in length from a quarter mile to a mile and a half, lace the property and probe its every corner. Where the land gets soft, soggy or downright wet, you can—from elevated boardwalks, a floating bridge, and observation towers—get close-up views of landscape and habitats not usually observable without hard walking and waterlogged boots. The variety and lushness of habitat, good cover, and abundant food sources all make for good birdwatching.

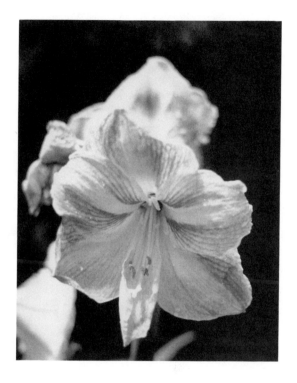

The Kent Intermediate School District, which owns the Howard Christian Nature Center, focuses its services and facilities on educating school children about nature and the environment. This is especially evident in the center's interpretive building, where several exhibits and learning stations help nurture an appreciation of nature's fascinating diversity and interdependence. Mammal and bird specimens are also set up for detailed study and examination. The interpretive center, which is open to the public, also houses a gift shop, book store and nature library.

County/City: Kent/Kent City

Fees: None.

Schedule: Hours for the interpretive center are 8 a.m. to 5 p.m., Monday through Friday. The grounds are always open.

Directions: From the junction of US-131 and M-46 in Cedar Springs, drive 6 miles west on M-46 (17 Mile Rd.) to Red Pine Dr. Turn right (north) onto Red Pine and drive 2.5 miles to the entrance.

Further Information: Howard Christian Nature Center, 16160 Red Pine Dr., Kent City, MI 49330; (616) 887-1852.

92 AMAN PARK

This Grand Rapids city park's quiet beauty, pleasant trails, and colorful array of plant life is the perfect antidote for a hectic lifestyle.

Beautiful Sand Creek winds through the heart of the park and dominates its landscape. The tiny creek almost ties itself in knots on its passage through Aman, and over the eons has carved a narrow, little valley that overlays the property with a large *S*.

You can get some impressive overlooks of the area from the park's three trails, which total nearly five miles. The paths dip in and out of the valley, cross the creek on two footbridges, skirt a tamarack bog and a small lake, and cut through a mature beech/maple forest and stands of aspen and hemlock.

No matter what the terrain—woods, fields or wetlands—the one constant at Aman is the brilliant and continual show of wildflowers from early spring through fall. Skunk cabbage and pussy willow herald spring in late March. Trout lily, marsh marigolds and Dutchman's breeches add their color to the surroundings in late April. And in May, violets, false Solomon's seal and many others burst into bloom. More flowers and brilliant berries continue the display through late summer and fall.

The wide diversity of food and shelter attract a fair number of birds throughout the year, with the peak of birding occurring during spring migration.

And in the winter—when most birds have headed south and the dry wildflowers are buried beneath a soft blanket of snow—cross country skiers take over the occasionally groomed trails.

County/City: Ottawa/Grand Rapids

Fees: None.

Schedule: Open all year.

Directions: From the intersection of I-196 and M-45 in Grand Rapids, go about 6 miles west on M-45 (Lake Michigan Ave.).

93　DAYTON WET PRAIRIE PRESERVE

This quietly spectacular preserve holds one of the last vestiges of a 15,000-acre prairie that at one time spread over much of the Michigan/Indiana border. The 47-acre parcel survived the plow and passed almost untouched into the hands of the Nature Conservancy because numerous small ponds and countless ground seepages made it unsuitable for farming. A jungle of wildflowers, however, thrives in the moist, rich soil.

No trails have made their way into the sanctuary, since most of the land is a checkerboard of small, relatively dry hummocks; wet, soggy depressions; and waist-high grass. About the only place from which to appreciate the colorful profusion of plant life is from Curran Road, which bisects the preserve from east to west. With a wildflower guide you can identify and photograph plants—including rare and threatened species such as rosin weed, Jacobs ladder, spotted phlox and numerous grasses—within a few feet of the road. The preserve area south of the road is higher and drier than the north, and you can walk several yards into and over the primeval prairie there.

County/City: Berrien/Buchanan
Fees: None.
Schedule: Open all year.
Directions: From the intersection of US-12 and US-31, drive west on US-12 approximately 2 miles to Red Bud Trail. Turn left (south) onto Red Bud and go 2 miles to Curran Rd. Turn right (west) onto Curran, drive approximately 2 miles to the preserve, and park in a small turnoff.

94 BERTRAND PARK

This heavily wooded 121-acre Berrien County park is as pleasing to the senses today as it must have been to the Indians who passed through it on the Sauk and Chicago trails and to the French voyageurs who paddled their fur-laden canoes down the historic St. Joseph River, which marks the park's west boundary.

Today, foot travelers in the park can follow the course of the slow-moving river for almost half a mile on a trail atop steep-sided bluffs that line the water. Other of the park's four-plus miles of scenic hiking routes skirt several open meadows and cut narrow corridors through a dense second-growth forest. Birding is excellent along all the paths, and sharp eyes and quiet steps may also reward you with glimpses of the deer that inhabit the park. For even more hiking options, you can take a trail that connects to Indiana's St. Patrick County Park, across Bertrand's south boundary. A detailed brochure, available at Bertrand's visitor center, maps the hiking trails in both parks and also highlights the Hoosier park's other facilities.

Madeline Bertrand Park is named after a Potawatomi woman, but the French traders called the area *Parc aux Vaches* ("cow pasture") because they regularly spotted buffalo grazing in a meadow here. Today, the pasture where buffalo roamed is a broad, grassy picnic grounds ringed by trees. Most tables and grills there are within easy walking distance of playgrounds, ball fields, hiking trails and the park's most unusual feature, an 18-hole disc golf course, where players use frisbee-like discs instead of balls and clubs to reach from tees to holes. Scattered throughout the park are several picnic shelters, including one built out over the side of a bluff with a commanding view of the 50-yard-wide St. Joseph River.

The visitor center is the staging area for a variety of nature programs, which range from night nature walks to fall color tours. A window wall on one side of the building looks out onto a bird feeding area.

During the winter months, you can cross country ski over 3.5 kilometers of groomed trails. Fires blaze in trailside warming shelters, and at night, torches line some of the tracks.

County/City: Berrien/Niles

Fees: County residents—$2 per vehicle daily, $15 annually; Non-residents—$3 per vehicle daily, $20 annually.

Schedule: Monday-Friday, 12 noon to 7 p.m.; Saturday and Sunday, 10 a.m. to 7 p.m.

Directions: From the intersection of US-12 and US-33, south of Niles, drive approximately 2 miles south on US-33 to Ontario Dr. Turn right (west) onto Ontario and drive 1/2 mile to where it deadends at Adams Rd. Turn left (south) onto Adams and drive less than 1/2 mile to the park entrance.

Further Information: Madeline Bertrand Park, 3038 Adams Rd., Niles, MI 49120; (616) 683-8280.

95 TRILLIUM RAVINE PLANT PRESERVE

It's just a short, pleasant stroll through a small stand of mature hardwoods to the focal point of this 15-acre Michigan Nature Association parcel. Problem is, by late spring the walk passes through such a profusion of delicate beauty, you may have trouble reaching the most memorable spot in the preserve.

So on your way to the main attraction, try to ignore the imposing, downright huge beech trees and don't get suckered into kneeling among the riot of wildflowers everywhere underfoot. Press on through all this natural beauty until you get to a *V*-shaped ravine with almost geometrically perfect sides. By late spring its steep slopes are blanketed in a rich, dense green that from a distance looks like the felt covering on a pool table. The panoramic view is captivating, but a closer look is what you're here for.

Covering the ravine's slopes are two flowers seldom found in Michigan—toadshade and prairie trillium. These wildflowers, which bloom as early as April 9th, have dark-red stalkless flowers that rest directly on the deep-green mottled leaves. Their rarity, exquisite beauty, and unusual setting in the ravine combine to make this tiny corner of the state a uniquely beautiful spot.

Once you have soaked in the view and studied the flowers, you can turn to the preserve's other treasures. Basswood, ironwood and red oak share the forest with beech and maple. Closer to the ground, mosses and ferns are scattered among wildflowers. In late spring, May-apples, violets, yellow trout lilies, wood poppies and other wildflowers grow so thick that it's almost impossible to walk the preserve without stepping on them.

County/City: Berrien/Niles

Fees: None.

Schedule: Open all year.

Directions: Drive north out of Niles on Business US-31 approximately 3 miles to US-31 (Walton Rd.). Turn left (west) onto Walton and drive west then south 0.8 miles to Geyer Rd. Turn left (east) onto Geyer and go 0.6 miles to the preserve, on the right-hand side of the road.

Further Information: Michigan Nature Association, 7981 Beard Rd., Box 102, Avoca, MI 48006.

96 RUSS FOREST PARK

At this Cass County park, you have the rare opportunity to picnic, hike, and study nature in a National Natural Landmark that also serves as a living research laboratory. The 10-acre park occupies a small corner of Newton Woods, one of the few stands of original Eastern hardwood forest left in Michigan. Dominated by sugar maple, beech and a few monstrous tuliptrees, Newton Woods' 580 acres contains a significant portion of all that remains of the rich broad-leaf forests that covered much of southern Michigan before the coming of European settlers. The woods are owned by the Forestry Department of Michigan State University, and scattered through the ancient woods are demonstration plantings, tree plantations, and research areas where scientists are studying the natural process of the forest and developing methods for improving forest management.

But you don't have to be a scientist to appreciate or enjoy the area. You can hike three trails, ranging from one to slightly more than a mile and a half in length, that pass underneath towering stands of old-growth hardwoods, cross a picturesque trout stream, lead to a log cabin, and take in a variety of interesting tree plantations. Within a short walk of the east entrance, for instance, a white-pine stand planted in 1945 and a grove of black walnut, white ash, red oak and black cherry planted in 1946 edge the trail. Other specimen trees are labeled along the routes.

The biggest tuliptree east of the Mississippi grew here until blown down in 1984 by a great storm. A 16-foot section of that 400-year-old monster is on display near the park's east entrance, and you can see its stump at the end of an 0.8-mile trail. Close to it is a living relative that some day may inherit the downed giant's title.

At the park's east entrance, a small picnic grounds and pavilion nestles beside a sparkling, little creek. A much bigger picnic area, with a large playground and pavilion, hides beneath the forest canopy of a dense grove of hardwoods on

the other side of the creek. A road from the west entrance circles through those deeply shaded grounds, and you'll find individual parking spots next to most tables and grills. A short path and wood bridge that crosses the stream join the two picnic areas.

County/City: Cass/Marcellus

Fees: None.

Schedule: Open all year.

Directions: From Marcellus, go about 8 miles west on Marcellus Highway.

Further Information: Cass County Parks Dept., 340 N. O'Keefe St., Cassopolis, MI 49031.

97 LAWLESS COUNTY PARK

If you think that our state's southern tier of counties are rather flat and featureless, this Cass County park will pleasantly surprise you. A covey of nobby hills and deep hollows ripple the park's landscape. Open fields dot the grounds, but a dense hardwood forest covers most of the park. Two small lakes, a pond and a stream that hide amid the folds and depressions add their charm to the landscape.

The park's four trails all begin and end in the central parking area, and their long, leisurely loops trace a giant four-leaf clover across the property. The nearly four miles of wide, well-marked paths involve plenty of up and down walking as they cut through the heart of the wooded hills, cross the stream, and lead to both Hogback and Doane lakes. Trail maps are available at the park entrance and the County Road Commission office, 340 North O'Keefe Street, Cassopolis.

The combination of deep cover, open fields and sheltered lakes holds out the promise of good birdwatching. Deer are plentiful, and if you walk quietly and keep a sharp lookout, you're likely to spot more than one whitetail moving through the woods.

A picnic area and pavilion borders the parking lot, and there's plenty of room on nearby fields for ballgames and other group activities. Future plans call for developed ball diamonds and a handicap-access nature trail.

In winter, intermediate through advanced cross country skiers set tracks on the wide paths, and a snowmobile trail ribbons a remote corner of the park. Kids especially love the manmade tubing hill, and the park even supplies the tubes.

County/City: Cass/Vandalia

Fees: $1 per car daily.

Schedule: Open sunrise to sunset year round.

Directions: From Vandalia, drive 2 miles east on M-60 to Lewis Lake Rd. Turn right (south) onto Lewis and drive 0.8 miles to Monkey Run St. Turn left (east) onto Monkey and drive 1/2 mile to the park entrance.

98 COVERED BRIDGE COUNTY PARK

Although this St. Joseph County park is named after the Langley Covered Bridge, which is visible about a half mile upstream, it's the Sturgis Dam and the impounded waters of the St. Joseph River that give the 15-acre park its distinctive flavor. The backwaters of the river sculpt the park's shoreline into gentle loops and curves, create a succession of small ponds and marshy wetlands on its west end, and provide a scenic vista for diners from almost any vantage point in the picnic area.

The grassy, tree-shaded picnic grounds lines the water in back of the dam and curves around a small half-moon inlet. Tables and grills are only a few steps from the parking lot, and, in many cases, are just yards from the water's edge. Some of the tables and grills, plus a playground, fill up a small tree-covered peninsula that extends out into the impoundment.

Judging from the number of fishing lines and lures draped from the picnic grounds' trees and occasional power lines, visitors use the area as much for catching dinner as eating it.

Upriver from the picnic area, a short but scenic nature trail winds through a stand of lowland hardwoods, edges quiet swamps and marshes, and takes birders, hikers and wildflower enthusiasts over narrow sloughs on weathered footbridges. Another path leads out onto Sturgis Dam, where the water laps the shore at your very feet on the east, while on the west the dry earthen dam falls away to a large rush-filled marsh almost 30 feet below the level of the impoundment.

The abundant cover and diverse landscape should attract a wide variety of birdlife throughout the year, making this a potentially prime birding spot.

County/City: St. Joseph/Mendon

Fees: None.

Schedule: Open all year.

Directions: From Mendon, drive 3 miles west on M-60 to Silver St. Turn left (south) onto Silver and drive 3.4 miles to the covered bridge. Immediately after crossing the bridge, turn right and drive 1/2 mile to the park.

99 PAHL POINT PARK

⋏ ⋔

On the face of it, this small St. Joseph County park hardly seems worth going out of your way to visit. At three acres in size and with only three picnic tables, it doesn't appear to have much to offer. But if you want to experience small slices of diverse habitat without large expenditures of energy, if you like to picnic in private, or if you're after maximum bird sightings with minimum effort, this vest-pocket park will suit you just fine. And there's an added bonus: You get a striking view of one of only two historic covered bridges in the state, only a short walk away.

The park's lone nature trail can hardly be more than 100 yards long, but within that distance it cuts through a small stand of mature hardwoods, bisects a reedy wetlands and tiny marsh, and takes you out onto a dock that extends into a backwater of the St. Joseph River formed by the Sturgis Dam. On the brief walk, you'll pass a fine sampling of wildflowers and native Michigan plants and move through an area with good birding possibilities. The extensive open water attracts waterfowl, the dense marsh and brush edging the backwater draws other species, and the woods and open fields surrounding the park shelter even more varieties.

The picnic grounds, with its three tables and grills, flanks the nature area, and you can almost always be assured of having the place to yourself.

Visible from the dock at the end of the nature trail and only a couple of hundred yards walk from the park entrance on Silver St. is the Langley Covered Bridge. Built in 1887, the old, red structure with white trim is the longest covered bridge in the state.

County/City: St. Joseph/Mendon

Fees: None.

Schedule: Open year round.

Directions: From Mendon, drive 3 miles west on M-60 to Silver St. Turn left (south) onto Silver and drive 3.3 miles to the park entrance.

100 JENNEY WOODS PRESERVE

If you don't like to be restricted to well-worn paths or be guided through natural areas by signs and guideposts, this Nature Conservancy preserve will suit you to a tee. The wild, untamed 142-acre tract of swamp, old-growth hardwoods and swamp forest has no trails, no interpretive signs, no restroom and no parking lot. In fact the only concession to visitors is a sign that lets you know you've found the preserve.

To get into the sanctuary, you have to shoulder your way through a dense understory of young trees, tall grass and shrubs. Once in the preserve, which fronts C Road for several hundred yards and fans out to the south, you are free to wander to your heart's content or until your stamina gives out. Be sure to take a compass, however, because it's easy to become disoriented, especially deep into the area.

A stand of mature silver maple and oaks somehow escaped the axe and have grown to truly impressive dimensions on 20 acres of Jenney Woods. The preserve is also home to a variety of animals and birds, including Acadian Flycatchers and Cerulean Warblers, which are at the extreme northern limits of their range in Calhoun County.

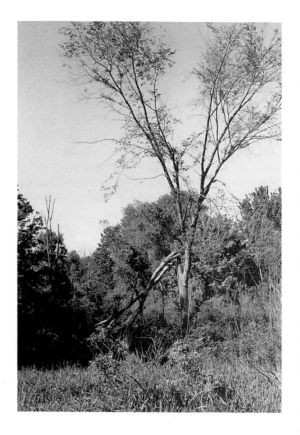

County/City: Calhoun/Marshall

Fees: None.

Schedule: Open all year.

Directions: From the I-69/I-94 interchange, drive south on I-69 approximately 6 miles to F Drive South. Go west on F Drive less than 1/2 mile to 15 1/2 Mile Rd. Turn right (north) onto 15 1/2 Mile and go 1.5 miles to C Drive. Turn left (west) and drive 3 miles to the preserve.

101 BROCK PARK

This forest-shrouded Ionia County park hugs busy highway M-21, but most motorists zip by, only aware of its presence if they spot the entrance sign. Those in the know turn off M-21 and slip under the canopy of thick, towering hardwoods and evergreens that shelter a sprawling, secluded campground and a beautiful picnic area bisected by a bright, swift-moving stream.

The park road snakes through the deep forest and skirts openings in the woods that are sprinkled with picnic tables and grills. Nearly all picnic spots are private and shady, and many are within sight and sound of the stream. Two picturesque fieldstone footbridges that arch over the stream lead to exceptionally private picnic areas, tennis courts, and the start of the park's nature trail.

The trail begins at a staircase that climbs a steep hill trapped within a narrow loop of the creek, and from the top of the stairs, you can work your way along the ridge of the high, thin finger of land. The valley falls steeply away from both sides of the trail, and sharp-edged gullies score the sides of the hill. Near the "finger's" tip, the trail forces you to turn around and retrace your steps to the trailhead.

Other faint, unmarked trails head every which-way through the park and include several that edge the stream.

In the winter nine miles of track-set cross country ski trails lace the hilly terrain.

At the park's primitive camping area, you can choose from plenty of scenic and secluded spots to set up. The campground road is, itself, quite scenic as it winds up and down hills and around hairpin curves in a dense old-growth forest dotted with small openings that can hold a single tent or trailer. Dozens of yards of deep woods often separate the sites, which means you'll have both privacy and shade.

County/City: Ionia/Ionia

Fees: $1 per car daily for county residents, $2 per car daily for non-residents.

Schedule: Open all year.

Directions: From Ionia go 3 miles west on M-21.

102   FOX PARK

Activity at this 35-acre Eaton County park centers around a long, narrow manmade lake. A beach—which edges the west side of the small, oblong body of water—is backed by a gently rising grassy area, where swimmers and sunbathers can spread their blankets and parents can keep a sharp eye on their children. At the top of the hill, a large playground overlooks the grassy slope and water. On the opposite shore, a picnic grounds reaches down to the lake, and shore fishermen can try their luck at several spots around the water's edge.

Two miles of hiking trails all begin near the picnic area. One that makes the less than one mile

trip around the lake is good for little more than exercise. The paths that slip into the woods that guard the back of the picnic area, however, reveal an interesting mix of wildflowers, flowering shrubs, some impressively large hardwoods, and a diverse forest landscape. One trail, just east of the picnic area, crosses a low, wet forested area on an elevated boardwalk with closeup views of swamps typical of those that covered much of Michigan before settlers cleared the timber and drained the land. North of the lake, another trail borders a quiet tree-lined pond that is home to turtles, frogs, and occasional ducks and herons. On all trails walking is easy over gently rolling terrain, and the woods are lovely in spring, summer and fall.

In the winter, cross country skiers can explore the same landscape on two miles of soft, groomed trails.

County/City: Eaton/Potterville

Fees: $2 daily permit, $12 annual permit; $6 senior citizen annual permit.

Schedule: Open all year.

Directions: From the intersection of I-69/US-27 and M-100 in Potterville, go north on M-100 one mile to Gresham Hwy. Turn left (west) onto Gresham and drive less than a mile to the park entrance.

Further Information: Eaton County Parks and Recreation, 3808 Grand Ledge Hwy., Grand Ledge, MI 48837.

The Rose Lake Wildlife Research Center is one of the most underrated and overlooked great birdwatching areas in the state. The Department of Natural Resources purchased the 3,334-acre tract in the 1930s for use as a research station and management area to study farm-habitat wildlife.

The center's rolling farmland, old fields, upland and lowland woods, brushy areas, wetlands and five lakes offer plenty of food and shelter to a wide variety of birds. And man has improved upon nature's work by creating ponds, flood areas, brush piles, and tree and shrub plantings to make the area even more attractive to wildlife. The work has obviously paid off, because the center's checklist numbers 228 bird species observed here since 1960. The impressive list includes more than 30 kinds of warblers, six species of woodpeckers, 23 varieties of ducks and geese, and nesting Sandhill Cranes. The handy checklist, available at the headquarters building, also notes each species' abundance and rates the likelihood of spotting them during each season.

You'll also want to pickup up the brochure, "Mammals of Rose Lake Wildlife Research Area," and then keep your eyes peeled for the 41 mammals—from masked shrews and silver-haired bats to red fox and long-tailed weasels—found in the area. The annotated list tells where you're most likely to spot each animal, how abundant or rare it is in the area, and a bit of its natural history.

Rose Lake has no dedicated hiking trails, but you can choose from plenty of short or long walks along several narrow work roads that wind through the landscape. Also, public roads that crisscross the area provide good vantage points for birding. A free detailed map of the research center, also available at the headquarters building, clearly marks all work roads and points out parking lots where you can leave your car and explore the area on foot.

The center is also open to hunters, fishermen and cross country skiers and contains both a rifle and skeet range.

County/City: Clinton/East Lansing

Fees: None.

Schedule: Open all year.

Directions: From I-69 approximately 12 miles northeast of Lansing, exit onto Business I-69 (exit 94). Immediately after exiting turn east onto old M-78 and drive 1/2 mile to Upton Rd. Turn left (north) onto Upton and go 1.5 miles to Stoll Rd. Turn right (east) onto Stoll and go 1/4 mile to the headquarters building.

Further Information: Rose Lake Wildlife Research Center, 8562 E. Stoll Rd., East Lansing, MI 48823.

SOUTHEASTERN
LOWER PENINSULA

104 BAKER WOODLOT

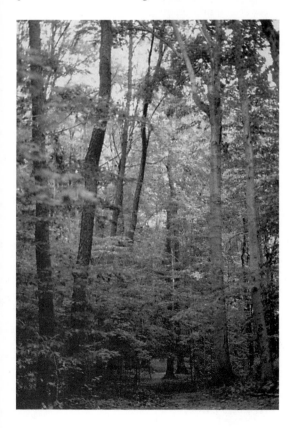

Michigan State University's 173-acre Baker Woodlot holds a soul-stirring fragment of the great beech/maple climax forest that once blanketed much of southern Michigan. Imposing specimens of oak, basswood, ash, cherry, maple, beech, tuliptree and elm compete for space and a piece of the sky everywhere you look. Many of the largest trees are between 100 and 150 years old, and a few grand, old elms have been around for 300 years. Some visitors say they feel almost reverent when they walk beneath the trees, which have stood in silent witness to the passing of so much human and natural history.

You can easily experience the sanctuary by hiking any of several wide, level paths that circle its perimeter and cut through the heart of the forest.

Five major ponds and several seasonal swamps add variety to the landscape, and be sure to bring tree and plant guides to help identify the 357 species of vascular plants that grow here.

Baker Woodlot, the largest natural area on the MSU campus, has not escaped unscathed over the years from the intrusion of man. Selective timber cutting has occurred, some species foreign to the area have been introduced, and the construction of a drainage ditch across a corner of the natural area has altered, to some degree, the natural evolution of the forest. Although that may detract somewhat from the scientific value of the area, it's all but undetectable to most of us, who simply wish to savor the magnificence of a mature woods. And Baker Woodlot *is* protected from further intentional alteration by man.

County/City: Ingham/East Lansing

Fees: None.

Schedule: Open all year.

Directions: From Grand River Ave. in East Lansing, turn south onto Hagadorn Rd. and go approximately 1/2 mile to Service Rd. Turn west (right) onto Service and drive approximately 3/4 mile to Farm Ln. Turn left (south) onto Farm Ln. and park on the shoulder of the road near the entrance gate to the woodlot, just south of the intersection on the east side of Farm Ln.

Southeastern Lower Peninsula

105 BEAL BOTANICAL GARDEN

You would expect one of the nation's premier agricultural colleges to have an impressive botanical garden. But 5,000 different kinds of plants artfully arranged in hundreds of carefully tended beds in just five acres?! W. J. Beal Garden, located in the heart of the Michigan State University campus, is a living tribute to a long line of talented gardeners and botanists. It is beautiful, peaceful, fascinating and, no matter how hard you try, impossible to take in or fully appreciate in just one visit. If you looked at each type of plant for just one minute, it would take more than 83 hours to see them all. But even a brief visit will bring you into contact with a surprising number and variety of growing things from all over the world.

The plant collections are organized into four broad categories. In one, families of plants are systematically arranged according to botanical relationships. Don't understand this category? Don't worry, the other three groupings make more

sense. The economic group features plants of direct use to humans, such as for food, fiber, perfume and medicine. That grouping also includes plants that are dangerous to people. Native Michigan plants make up another collection, and the last broad grouping showcases ornamental and landscape plants. Most specimens are accompanied by small signs that give the plant name and its history and habitat.

There are no formal paths through the garden, but you are free to stroll across the lush lawn from one rank of beds to another. One of the joys of Beal is the tight-packed variety. You can move only a few steps from a zucchini to a coffee plant, black gum tree or Rose of Sharon, then turn again and come face to face with a weeping maidenhair tree, at 150 million years old, one of the two most ancient tree species still in existence. And from the exotic to the practical, the many shrubs, perennials and annuals will trigger gardening and landscaping ideas for your own yard.

If you need a break from bending over to find out the name of yet another strange plant, an ideal place to sit and enjoy this enclave of pastoral beauty, which has enchanted visitors since its founding in 1873, is at a goldfish pond near the center of the garden.

County/City: Ingham/East Lansing

Fees: None.

Schedule: Open dawn to dusk year round. However, during the academic year, approximately September through May, it's best not to visit on weekdays, when parking is at a premium.

Directions: In East Lansing, from the junction of E. Michigan Ave. and Grand River Ave., drive east on Grand River about one block to the Abbot Entrance to the MSU campus. Turn right (south) and go about one block to West Circle Dr. Make your way to the south part of the West Circle Dr. loop. Beal Gardens is just east of the intramural sports building and across from the music building. On weekends parking is available on West Circle Drive.

106 SANFORD NATURAL AREA

Squeezed between the bustling Michigan State University campus on the south and a commercial strip bordering Grand River Avenue on the north is an exceptional wilderness area. Take one step off the sidewalk on Hagadorn Road, which marks the Sanford Natural Area's east side, and you enter a hardwood forest of towering trees the likes of which covered much of lower Michigan before the coming of Europeans.

And this remnant of native Michigan forest will remain untouched. Sanford is one of a few spots on the MSU campus that are managed at "the highest level of protection and the lowest level of use." A Campus Natural Areas Committee must approve any collecting or other scientific study by professors, and class projects are limited to observation only. In addition, all downed trees are left where they fall, and there is no control of insects or poisonous plants within the natural area's boundaries.

As a result, at Sanford Natural Area and a few other locations on campus (see Baker Woodlot, p. 105, and Red Cedar Natural Area, p. 108), you can come closer to experiencing the untouched splendor of a natural forest stuck smack dab in a major urban setting than in any other large city in the state.

Broad, easily walked paths circle the area and penetrate to the heart of the dark, quiet woods. The Red Cedar River forms Sanford's 3,000-foot north boundary, and the abrupt border between the trees and moving water creates the most-memorable scenery in the preserve. Old cedars and gnarled, aging hardwoods lean out over the water. In many instances the current has undercut the trees to expose crazy latticeworks of huge roots over the water. Numerous exceptionally picturesque views come from a well-worn path that edges the river.

Sanford Natural Area holds the promise of good birdwatching, especially on the edges of the preserve and the area bordering the river. Belted

Kingfishers are common along the river, warblers stop in the woods during spring migration, and you can observe thrushes busily investigating the leaf-strewn forest floor.

County/City: Ingham/East Lansing

Fees: None.

Schedule: Open all year.

Directions: The preserve is on the west side of Hagadorn Rd. across the Red Cedar River, just south of Grand River Ave. Parking can be a problem. On weekends you can park in the North Hubbard Hall lot, on Hagadorn Rd. south of the preserve. During the week it's best to park off Grand River Ave. near Hagadorn Rd. and walk to the preserve.

107 RED CEDAR NATURAL AREA

The Red Cedar and Sanford (see p. 107) natural areas are wilderness outposts that guard the west and east flanks of beautiful Michigan State University. They are nearly twins. Both are covered by towering hardwoods, and the Red Cedar River defines their north boundaries. Both are managed at a high level of protection and low level of use. That is, visitors are allowed to wander the preserve, but all other activities, including scientific research, must be approved by a Campus Natural Areas Committee. Both are primal sanctuaries that stand in silent tribute to the great forests that covered southern Michigan before they were cleared by farmers and lumbermen.

But the Red Cedar Natural Area—because it's much less accessible and, thus, less frequently used—seems much more remote and wild. There are no marked entrances to the natural area, not even a sign identifying its existence. To explore the preserve, park alongside Kalamazoo Street near the bridge that crosses the Red Cedar River and enter the forest on either side of the road. The paths are not well-defined, but that adds to the feeling of the area's untouched uniqueness.

Birdwatching possibilities along the edges of the forest and near the river are excellent.

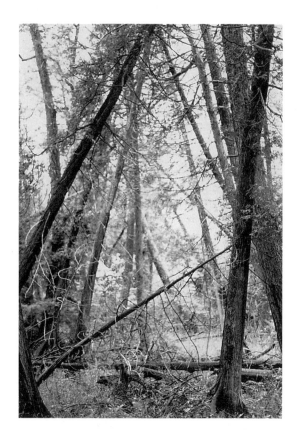

County/City: Ingham/East Lansing

Fees: None.

Schedule: Open all year.

Directions: From the intersection of Michigan Ave. and Grand River Ave. in East Lansing, go 2 blocks west on Michigan to Harrison Rd. Turn (left) south onto Harrison and drive one block to Kalamazoo St. Turn right (west) onto Kalamazoo, drive approximately 1/2 mile, and park on the shoulder of the road just before Kalamazoo crosses the river.

108 PINE HAVEN RECREATION AREA

Every September the Pine Haven Recreation Area hosts the Mud Creek Crawl, a footrace that *Runner's World* magazine lists as one of the nation's top 13 Out-of-the-Way Races. So what does that have to do with nature and nature lovers? The reason the magazine rates the race so highly is because of its beautiful and unusual surroundings, and that's of definite interest to hikers and cross country skiers.

Eight wooded trails—with intriguing names like Logger's Flats, Mud Creek Loop, Riverside Ravine, and Oxbow Flats—cut through the dense upland forest of second-growth pine, birch and hardwoods that covers this 325-acre Midland County Park. The generally flat landscape is interrupted by low sand ridges that mark the shoreline of an ancient great lake and also by the narrow flood plain valley of the Salt River and Mud Creek, both of which flow through the park.

The wide, well-marked trails, which range in length from 0.7 to 2.3 miles, are beautiful year round. Wildflowers mat the forest floor in the spring and give way to feathery ferns dappled by shadows in the summer. In the fall the trails are dark lines drawn through an avant-garde canvas of bright colors formed by fallen leaves. And in winter, dark, leafless trunks rise out of the snow in sharp contrast to the blanket of white.

With a little imagination, you can combine the eight miles of interconnected pathways into an outing tailored to your skill and stamina. Trail markers indicate degree of difficulty to cross country skiers, and hikers can also use them to determine the amount of exertion required to traverse the various routes. For skiers, green circles identify beginning trails, blue squares mark ones of intermediate level, and black diamonds indicate those for experts.

A descriptive brochure that includes a trail map is usually available at the trailhead. A map of the entire system is also posted at the trailhead and at all trail intersections.

County/City: Midland/Sanford

Fees: None for hiking; donations are requested for trail grooming in the winter.

Schedule: Open during daylight hours year round.

Directions: From US-10 approximately 7 miles northwest of Midland, exit onto West River Rd and drive south a few hundred feet to Maynard Rd. Turn right (west) onto Maynard and drive one mile to the park entrance.

Further Information: Dept. of Parks and Recreation, Midland County Services Bldg., 220 W. Ellsworth St., Midland, MI 48640.

Southeastern Lower Peninsula

109 VETERANS MEMORIAL PARK

Hiding in a small corner of this sprawling Midland County park is one of the state's rarest and most precious natural treasures—one of only four known stands of virgin white pine in the Lower Peninsula. An added plus: It takes little effort to walk among the majestic, awe-inspiring giants that have been reaching for the sky since the presidency of James Monroe.

Just steps from the park entrance, the quarter-mile-long Veterans Memorial Trail plunges into a world untouched by man. The circular, bark-covered path crosses a creek, then borders a deep, narrow ravine. It is on the edge of this ravine that the huge 170-year-old white pine and virgin red pine rise from the needle-strewn ground and punch through a green canopy spread by lesser trees. It's a unique piece of natural architecture, as though the leafy roof is being supported by huge Greek columns. You could walk the trail non-stop in 10 minutes, but that's nearly impossible once you're amidst the jaw-dropping splendor.

The mile-long Upland Trail, though it bypasses the dramatic virgin pines, does lead to a variety of other interesting natural features as it loops through the park's lower half. The easily walked path crosses a pretty stream, skirts vernal ponds (pools created by melting winter snow and spring rain that dry up in the summer), tunnels through deep woods, and climbs over low sand ridges that mark the shoreline of a prehistoric great lake that preceded present-day Lake Huron.

A self-guiding brochure to both trails is available at the park entrance. Numbered stops along the routes correspond to numbered paragraphs that describe the park's natural features, identify various trees and vegetation, tell the natural history of the area, and explain how man and nature interact. The Veterans Trail has eight stops, and the Upland Trail, with 30 stops, can easily take an hour to walk. You are also free to bushwhack into the completely undeveloped wilderness that makes up the park's northern half.

Picnic tables and grills are widely scattered amid stately hardwoods and pines in the southern half of the park. It's only a short walk from almost any of the picnic sites to the trailheads or also to a canoe launch on the Salt River, which crosses the park's eastern boundary. From that put-in it's only a quarter-mile float to the Salt's juncture with the Tittabawassee River and from there a scenic four-hour paddle to downtown Midland.

County/City: Midland/Midland

Fees: None.

Schedule: Memorial Day to Labor Day, 7 a.m. to dusk; rest of the year, 8 a.m. to dusk.

Directions: From US-10 approximately 7 miles northwest of Midland, take the West River Rd. exit and go south on West River Rd. one mile to Saginaw Rd. Turn left (east) onto Saginaw and drive 1/4 mile to Seven Mile Rd. Turn right (south) onto Seven Mile and drive 1/4 mile to Cole Rd. Turn right (west) onto Cole and drive 1/2 mile to Neiner Rd. Turn right (north) onto Neiner and drive one block to the park entrance.

Further Information: Dept. of Parks and Recreation, Midland County Services Bldg., 220 W. Ellsworth St., Midland, MI 48640.

110 SANFORD LAKE PARK

For those who like to spend the afternoon bellied up to a picnic table savoring the special flavor that only cooking and eating outside can impart to food, Sanford Lake rates as a four-star eatery. All you need for a full day of pleasure here is a picnic basket or cooler and maybe a blanket. But there's more—a boat launching ramp for pleasure boaters and fishermen and a nice swimming beach.

Sanford's huge picnic area is set amidst a forest of pine, birch and maple, and the trees are close enough together that most sites are fairly private. You can choose a table close to the scenic beauty of Sanford Lake or stake a claim to a more secluded spot well back from the water. What you can't do is find an unattractive place to eat.

Hundreds of swimmers and sunbathers can comfortably use the beach, which curves along the lakeshore for 1,100 feet. At both ends of the park, the sand narrows to a relatively thin band, but at the center, where a large bathhouse and concession stand overlook the lake, the beach spreads dozens of yards back from the water line.

Two large playgrounds should siphon off whatever energy young people have left after wading, swimming and playing in the sand.

County/City: Midland/Sanford

Fees: County residents $3 daily; non-residents $4 daily.

Schedule: May 1-Labor Day, 8 a.m. to 10 p.m.; rest of the year, 8 a.m. to dusk.

Directions: From US-10 approximately 7 miles northwest of Midland, take the West River Rd. exit and drive south on West River Rd. 1/2 mile to Irish Rd. Turn left (east) onto Irish and drive 1/4 mile to the park entrance.

Further Information: Dept. of Parks and Recreation, Midland County Services Building, 220 W. Ellsworth St., Midland, MI 48640.

Southeastern Lower Peninsula

111   CROW ISLAND STATE GAME AREA

Each year thousands of amateur and hundreds of dedicated birders literally drive right over this excellent birdwatching area without realizing it's there. The high retaining walls of the new Zilwaukee Bridge, which carries I-75 over the Saginaw River, barely allows a glimpse of the more than 1,000-acre state game area that stretches along the river from the foot of the bridge to Bay City. But the last exit before crossing the bridge from the south leads to a 1.5-mile-long strip of highway M-13 from which you can potentially spot thousands of birds.

The entire Crow Island State Game Area serves as a giant overflow basin for Michigan's largest watershed, and what's not perpetually covered with water is usually wet at some time during the year. M-13 runs along the east bank of the Saginaw River, which divides the preserve into east and west sections. An immense dike circles the 300-plus-acre east unit, which consists mostly of a huge cattail sedge, marsh and occasional open ponds. Public access is not permitted in that area, which is just as well since walking there would be impossible. But the wide shoulders of M-13 make a great platform for birding. And don't direct all your attention to the marsh, because the river attracts more than its fair share of birds.

An astonishing number of waterfowl and shorebirds stop over, feed and nest in the state game area. Gulls and terns seem ever-present, and you can often spot ducks and geese by the hundreds. Wood Ducks, American Black Ducks, Mallards, Blue-winged Teal, Northern Pintails, Gadwall, Canvasbacks, Green-winged Teal, and Redhead, Bufflehead and Ruddy ducks are all commonly sighted. Tundra Swans make biannual stops in spring and fall, and Ospreys, Bald Eagles, Northern Harriers and Red-shouldered Hawks pay occasional visits. Among the shorebirds that frequent the marshy fringes are Black-crowned Night Herons, American Bitterns, Great Egrets, Great Blue Herons, Green Herons, Willets, Snowy Egrets,

Soras and Virginia Rails.

That's not a bad day of birding without ever having to leave your car. The best times, of course, for spotting the greatest number and variety are during spring and fall migrations.

County/City: Saginaw/Saginaw

Fees: None.

Schedule: None.

Directions: The game area is immediately east of I-75 on M-13. To reach it, take take exit 153 from I-75.

112 IMERMAN MEMORIAL PARK

Imerman Memorial Park combines the best features of an old-fashioned county park with those of a new multi-facility recreation area. And what's more, it's a great place for nature lovers.

Its clean, well-maintained picnic grounds are the kind that city folks have chosen for generations as a place to enjoy an outdoor meal. Tables and grills are widely spaced across a sprawling, sun-drenched lawn, and families and other large groups can spread out around a chosen spot without crowding others or being crowded.

Those who want more than a traditional summer picnic have an almost unlimited choice of year-round facilities including baseball diamonds, a large children's playground, basketball courts, canoe rentals, a boat launching ramp, a fishing dock, a volleyball court, shuffleboard courts, tennis courts, horseshoe pits and cross country ski trails.

You can also enjoy a quiet, solitary experience with nature by walking the Floodplain Forest Trail, a 1.25-mile self-guiding nature/hiking path that circles the entire park. Eight stops along the route are keyed to an interpretive booklet, available at the park entrance, that explains how forest regeneration, wildlife, and the work of natural forces all affect the park's landscape. For instance, the entire trail lies in the flood plain of the Tittabawassee, and seasonal floods in spring and fall occasionally place the trail and park at the bottom of a suddenly expanded river.

For more than half its distance, the trail borders the historic Tittabawassee River. In the 1800s this river, which flowed through an area rich in pine forests, served as a water highway for transporting millions of logs to sawmills that lined the Saginaw River. Old pilings, still visible in the water, are the last remnants of massive booms that collected the logs before they were floated to the mills and turned into lumber.

The park's variety of habitat and cover—which includes open meadows, a grove of giant cotton-woods, dense brush, moving water, and many areas of transition from woods to fields—attracts numerous birds and should prove fruitful to birdwatchers.

The river's water quality has improved in recent years and so has the fishing. Spring and fall anglers pull walleyes from the water, and white bass, channel catfish and bullheads provide the majority of the action the rest of the year.

Cross country skiers glide around the park on two trails in the winter, and recreation and nature programs are conducted at Imerman throughout the year.

County/City: Saginaw/Saginaw

Fees: $1.50 per car daily.

Schedule: Open all year, 8 a.m. to 9 p.m.

Directions: From the intersection of M-47 and M-46 on the west side of Saginaw, drive approximately 4 miles north on M-47.

Further Information: Saginaw County Parks, County Governmental Center, Saginaw, MI 48602; (517) 790-5280.

113 HARTLEY OUTDOOR EDUCATION CENTER

Although this 200-acre Saginaw Intermediate School District nature center's primary function is to serve as an outdoor classroom and learning center for students, the general public is also more than welcome to stop by and explore this beautiful facility.

From the central activities building—which houses four classrooms, a dining room and a student dormitory—nearly a dozen trails fan out through the marshes, lowland forests, ponds, creek, open meadows and upland forest that make up the preserve. A combination of asphalt, woodchip, cinder, and bare-earth trails plus extensive boardwalks lead to virtually every corner of the sanctuary. The lengthy routes make for a variety of beautiful and enjoyable walks. One winding asphalt route is handicap accessible.

The area, which shelters a wide variety of flora and fauna, is also rich in human history, and along the trails you'll see a coal mine that operated from 1896 to 1936, an authentic reproduction of an Indian village, and a 100-year-old pioneer cabin.

The diversity of habitat plus spillover from a huge wetlands that rings the preserve are reasons that an estimated 200-plus species of birds have been sighted in the area. Spotting, photographing and detailed study of the birds is easy and comfortable from four blinds that have been strategically placed along the trails to overlook a pond, a creek, a woods and a meadow. Also, a Bluebird walk is among the center's regularly scheduled nature programs for the general public.

County/City: Saginaw/St. Charles

Fees: None.

Schedule: Open year round. During the school year it's best to call ahead to make sure that when you plan to visit there aren't several busloads of students using the faeilities and trails.

Directions: From downtown St. Charles go north on M-52 about 1/2 mile to North St. Turn left (west) onto North and drive 1/2 mile to Beaver Rd. Turn right (north) onto Beaver and drive 1/2 mile to the entrance.

Further Information: Hartley Outdoor Education Center, 12633 Beaver Rd., St. Charles, MI 48655; (517) 865-6295.

Waterfowl are some of Michigan's most beautiful birds, and their exquisite form, color and markings breed two insatiable obsessions. Once you get hooked on pursuing them with binoculars, you want to see more of them, and you want to see them up close. At the St. Charles Waterfowl Observatory, you can satisfy those passions.

There, from a 50-foot-diameter gazebo that encloses a small circular pond fed by a waterfall and surrounded by a covered walkway, you can sketch, photograph and study some of nature's most beautiful handiwork only a few feet away. Attached to the gazebo is a large, fenced-in breeding area where up to 30 pairs of waterfowl—including Canada Geese, Northern Shovelers, Wood Ducks, Green-wing Teal, and Pintail and Harlequin ducks—move among small pools and native Michigan plants. An especially interesting time to visit is during the spring breeding season, when the males preen and strut their stuff before the females. Decoy carvers find the observatory especially helpful in capturing the small details of waterfowl in wood.

The observatory, which sits on the west bank of the Bad River near downtown St. Charles, is surrounded by a vest-pocket-size area that is managed as a demonstration project for improving wildlife habitat. A short wood-chip-covered trail slips past the gazebo through that parcel of natural plantings to the river's edge.

County/City: Saginaw/St. Charles

Fees: None.

Schedule: Open daily from April 1 to November 30.

Directions: From downtown St. Charles go 1/4 mile north on M-52.

Further Information: Waterfowl, c/o Village of St. Charles, 110 W. Spruce St., St. Charles, MI 48655.

115 RINGWOOD FOREST

Man and nature forged a unique alliance to present us with unforgettable beauty at this 160-acre Saginaw County park. Like much of Saginaw Valley, this tract of land along the south branch of the Bad River was denuded of trees during the heyday of the lumbering era. But the children of the loggers who clear-cut the land here must have mourned the passing of the great trees, because in 1883 they began replanting the area. The result of this unusual love of land and foresight (it was one of the first reforestation projects in the state) is a lush, dark and almost mystical woods laced with miles of winding trails.

You can pick from six routes, which range from a gentle 0.4-mile round-trip stroll to 3.5 miles of up and down walking over the entire system. All trails start at the park's tree-shrouded picnic area.

Easily the most memorable trail is Spruce Alley, which follows a logging road through a virtual canyon formed by rows of giant spruce that line the path. Planted in 1883 by the son of Eleazer J. Ring, who first cleared the land, the trees are now among the oldest of their kind in Michigan.

Spruce Alley leads to Lumberjack Loop, a 1.1-mile trail that circles through the heart of the park. The route passes two scenic overlooks of the Bad River, and 14 numbered posts along the trail correspond to numbered paragraphs in an interpretive brochure that details the area's rich natural and human history. The pamphlet, available at the picnic grounds, also includes a handy identification key to 22 kinds of trees found in the park.

Other trails meander through the far reaches of the park. The longest route, the 1.8-mile Witch Hazel Trail, slips through a vast swamp and river flood plain before crossing the Bad River and climbing to higher ground.

At the picnic grounds, a stand of towering pines looms over the small pavilion, grills and tables, and the trees' fragrance will mix with the aroma of almost anything you cook.

A canoe launch site and bank fishing spots on the Bad River are only a short walk from the picnic area.

When snow flies, the trails here turn into some of the most demanding and beautiful cross country ski routes in the area.

County/City: Saginaw/St. Charles

Fees: None.

Schedule: Open all year.

Directions: From St. Charles go 2 miles south on M-52 to Ring Rd. Turn right (west) onto Ring and drive 2 miles to the entrance.

Further Information: Saginaw County Parks & Recreation Commission, County Government Center, Saginaw, MI 48602; (517) 790-5280.

If you could attribute human characteristics to nature areas, you'd call Brennan Nature Sanctuary "bashful". This 118-acre Michigan Nature Association parcel is surrounded by the unremarkable, tabletop-flat farmland of central St. Clair county; its existence is marked only by a small, simple and unobtrusive sign; and you have to walk at least a hundred yards into the preserve before it begins to reveal its unpretentious beauty. But once there, you'll fall in love with Brennan's untrampled and varied landscape, the wide variety of flora and fauna, and the peace and solitude.

A hundred yards east of Bricker Road, a glass-covered display case briefly describes the area's natural features, and from there a two-mile-long trail plunges into an impressive stand of red pine called Inspiration Grove. The tightly spaced, mature trees have softened the trail with a thick carpet of fallen needles. The narrow path emerges from the cool, quiet glade into an open meadow dotted with Bluebird boxes, and if you pause for only a few minutes, you'll usually be rewarded with the sighting of one of the delightful, beautiful birds. From the meadow the trail descends to the flood plain of the Pine River.

It's along the Pine, which can't seem to run in a straight line for more than a dozen yards before breaking into *S* curves, that the preserve is at its prettiest. Thick woods crowd the low banks and create a vaulted ceiling over the slow-moving water. In many places ferns cover the forest floor and add a lacey accent to the scene. Where the trees thin out, cattail marshes and swamps border the river.

You can walk the trail in under an hour, but you can also easily spend half a day seeking out and closely observing the profusion of plant and animal life. Michigan lilies, jewelweed, wild iris and numerous other wildflowers thrive in the sanctuary, and eastern hemlock, white spruce, white pine, balsam fir, beech and maple are among the many trees you'll find here.

Thirty-seven species make up the list of birds that have nested in the 118 acres. Warbling Vireos, Bob-o-links, Acadian Flycatchers, Red-eyed Vireos, Yellow Warblers and Northern Yellow-throat Warblers, in addition to Bluebirds, all raise young on the preserve. Those and the other nesting species, plus birds you might see during migration seasons, add up to some prime bird-watching opportunities.

County/City: St. Clair/Emmett

Fees: None.

Schedule: Open all year.

Directions: From I-69, exit onto M-19 and drive north about 2 miles to M-21. Turn right (east) onto M-21 and drive 1.8 miles to Bricker Rd. Turn left (north) onto Bricker and go 2 miles to the preserve sign, on the east side of the road. Park on the shoulder.

Further Information: Michigan Nature Association, 7981 Beard Rd., Box 102, Avoca, MI 48006.

117 TRILLIUM TRAIL NATURE PRESERVE

From the entrance to this Michigan Nature Association sanctuary, an easily walked, quarter-mile trail takes you to a secluded, undisturbed 21-acre pocket of unique natural beauty. The lightly used path descends to a valley, where brush that crowds the trail and imposing hardwoods draped with hanging vines effectively cut you off from sight and sound of the surrounding farms, homes and highways. On the valley floor, the trail crosses a small stream on a narrow footbridge, then begins to rise up the opposite side. Just before the trail climbs completely out of the valley and enters a meadow, a narrow footpath breaks off to the right and etches the edge of the steep hillside.

It is there that this preserve lives up to its name. Large-flowered white trillium—fairly rare now in

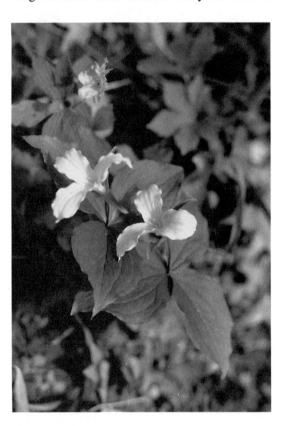

Michigan because of the disappearance of woodland where it thrives—blanket the hill. During the first three weeks of May when the trillium bloom, you can be treated to a magnificent display of white flowers cascading down the hillside. May apples, violets and numerous other flowers also splash color onto the scene. From the trail, the view of the long-undisturbed valley floor—filled with fallen trees, towering hardwoods and numerous shrubs—is equally impressive.

As evidenced by the nearly continuous symphony of singing and loud calling, birds especially like the shrubs and forest understory in the valley. It does, however, take both binoculars and patience to find them flitting around in the thick vegetation.

You can walk the entire preserve in 30 minutes, but don't be surprised if you end up spending hours searching for and identifying wildflowers or sitting on the hillside contemplating the beautiful lushness of the scenery.

County/City: St. Clair/Memphis

Fees: None.

Schedule: Open all year.

Directions: From Memphis, drive 1/4 mile north on M-19. Park on the shoulder of the road at the Michigan Nature Association sign (next to a Michigan highway sign) on the east side of the road, then walk east along the property line 1/4 mile to the sanctuary.

Further Information: Michigan Nature Association, 7981 Beard Rd., Box 102, Avoca, MI 48006.

118 HARSENS ISLAND

Whether you're touring the area or just studying it on a map, Harsens Island looks like it's 2,000 miles out of place. No one speaks Cajun here, you won't find Creole cooking, and there are no stilt houses. But the levees, dikes, mud flats, sometimes-indeterminate shoreline, open water, and wide expanse of grass-filled marshes seem like they should be part of the Mississippi Delta rather than Michigan's Lake St. Clair.

Harsens Island *is*, in fact, a part of a delta, but one formed by the St. Clair River and named the St. Clair Flats. For thousands of years, the river has taken in countless tons of sediment from the upper Great Lakes, carried it, then dropped its load when it emptied into Lake St. Clair. Those deposits of mud, sand, gravel and silt created a group of more than a dozen islands with convoluted shorelines that fit together as snugly as a jigsaw puzzle. The land is so low that in many places you can barely keep your feet dry. This complex and fascinating system of land, water, and areas that can't make up their mind which they are, is the largest delta in the Great Lakes.

Easiest to get to and easiest to see and see from is Harsen's Island. Its sheltered waters, sparse population and abundant wildlife make it a favored, no-frills recreation area for nature lovers.

Birdwatchers, including several Audubon clubs that make annual pilgrimmages, are drawn to Harsens in spring and fall to enjoy the large number and variety of waterfowl that call here on their way north and south. Birders don't have to work hard here. Roads that skirt the numerous marshes and border the many bays and inlets make excellent observation platforms. Swans, ducks, gallinules, terns, gulls and grebes dot the open water and, in many cases, paddle about their business only yards away from slowly moving cars. And if you're patient and careful, a search of the interior and along dense marshes that border many of the roads will turn up a wide assortment of marsh birds.

Harsens is also a great place to simply take a pleasant drive amid some of nature's most unique handiwork. The island's most striking and unusual physical feature is at its southern end. There, two long, low and narrow strips of land, separated by Little Muscamoot Bay, look like a pair of tails extending far out into Lake St. Clair.

A narrow gravel road traces the spine of each tail, and the roadbeds are, in many instances, the only high and dry land in a broad expanse of marsh and open water. Along the Middle Channel Drive, on the narrowest (west) tail, you come as close to boating on four wheels as it's possible to do without leaving a wake. Also, in places along that drive, the tail broadens to permit turnouts and at times even fattens enough to allow houses and cottages to be built on land virtually surrounded by water.

Other roads border the St. Clair Flats Wildlife Area, which covers almost half the island.

Not surprisingly, boaters and fishermen delight in the playground of bays, channels and sheltered backwaters. Twelve-foot bruised and battered aluminum fishing boats share the waterways with luxury motor yachts, sailboats of every description, and 600-foot-plus Great Lakes freighters and ocean-going ships.

The best views of the constant parade in the main shipping channel come from South Channel Drive, which follows the island's east shore.

County/City: St. Clair/Algonac

Fees: The 5-minute ferry ride costs $3.50 round trip per car.

Schedule: The ferry runs continuously, about every 10-15 minutes, year round.

Directions: The ferry to Harsens Island is less than 1/2 block west of M-29 in downtown Algonac. Look for the large sign.

From 1847 to 1967 the large, white building beside the north branch of the Clinton River was alive with the whir, roar and rumble of belts, pulleys, gears and giant grindstone, all kept in motion by the flow of the river over its water wheel. Today, except for the occasional soft tread of feet or the excited voices of visitors, the proud building stands silent, as a fitting centerpiece to the park that bears its name. The 2,380-acre Wolcott Mill Metropark not only puts you in touch with a piece of Michigan history, it's also a beautiful pastoral setting in which to enjoy nature and escape city life for a few hours.

The mill's huge rough-hewn timbers and clapboard siding enclose a variety of displays and exhibits that explain its history, operation and importance to area farmers. A bewildering number of machines, pulleys and chutes—all labeled—that turned grain into feed are particularly fascinating.

A little more than a quarter of a mile upriver from the mill is a dam and millrace that were built to channel water to the mill's power wheel. The construction of the old millrace—a long, straight ditch that parallels the river for several hundred yards—created a long, narrow island.

The Millrace Trail, an easily walked grass-covered interpretive pathway, circles that finger of land and leads to several pleasing views of the surrounding park land. From the mill, the trail borders the millrace, where you can look down inside at the numerous frogs and turtles that find shelter in the marsh grasses and shrubs that almost fill the long-unused channel. At the old dam, the trail reverses direction and, on its return to the mill, edges the banks of the shallow, swiftly moving Clinton River. The entire trip takes only about 20 minutes, but few walks of short duration provide such pleasant scenery.

Only 200 acres of the park is presently open to the public. But future development will open up even more land for recreational use, and an interpretive farm is also planned.

County/City: Macomb/Ray Center

Fees: None.

Schedule: Wolcott Mill Metropark is open May through October. Park Hours—Weekdays, 9 a.m.-5 p.m.; Weekends, 9 a.m.-7 p.m. Building Hours—Weekdays, 10 a.m.-5 p.m.; Weekends 10 a.m.-7 p.m.

Directions: From M-53, drive approximately 4.5 miles east on 29 Mile Rd. to Kunstman Rd. Turn left (north) onto Kunstman and drive 1/2 mile to the park entrance.

Further Information: Wolcott Mill Metropark, c/o Stony Creek Metropark, 4300 Main Park Rd., Washington, MI 48094.

Southeastern Lower Peninsula   120

120 WILCOX-WARNES MEMORIAL NATURE SANCTUARY

The Wilcox-Warnes Memorial Nature Sanctuary proves that nature, if left to its own devices, is more than capable of producing an arboretum the equal of any planned or nurtured by humans. More than 365 plant species grow at this 45-acre Michigan Nature Association preserve, and they're divided between two unequal and contrasting sections.

The northern 18 acres is a farm field that last felt a plow in 1957. Nature took over, and the old field is now undergoing plant succession. Small trees and shrubs crowd most of the acreage and compete for dominance.

The southern 27 acres has never been plowed or even grazed and, as a result, is covered by an impressive stand of old-growth hardwoods. Beech, red maple, white ash, oak, basswood, cherry, walnut, shagbark hickory and more than 400 tuliptrees grow in this part of the preserve. A small stream cuts across the southwest corner of the old woods, and a vernal pond fosters aquatic life in the spring.

Trillium, monkeyflower, bittersweet, May-apple and Jack-in-the-pulpit help make up an impressive collection of wildflowers. And the long list of shrubs and small trees includes sassafras, willow, prickly ash, serviceberry and flowering dogwood.

Bring a field guide to fully appreciate the amazing variety of plant life here. But you don't have to identify a single specimen to enjoy the abundant overall natural beauty that, because of the predominance of hardwoods, is especially memorable during fall color.

Narrow, easily walked trails crisscross the entire preserve, and the dense woods and underbrush shelter Woodcock, Ruffed Grouse, owls, hawks and songbirds. Deer tracks indent almost every piece of bare earth.

County/City: Macomb/Macomb

Fees: None.

Schedule: Open all year.

Directions: From M-53, drive 1.5 miles east on 26 Mile Rd. to Schoenherr Rd. Turn right (south) onto Schoenherr and go less than 0.2 mile to the entrance, marked by large rock on the west side of the road. Park on the shoulder of the road.

Further Information: Michigan Nature Association, 7981 Beard Rd., Box 102, Avoca, MI 48006.

Southeastern Lower Peninsula

The Sterling Heights Nature Center proves you don't always have to be in the out-of-doors to enjoy or appreciate nature. There are no established trails or even room for them at this seven-acre parcel, so the focus on nature here is in a cozy brick building that overlooks a large, grassy meadow on the Clinton River.

In one small exhibit wing, stuffed wildlife—including a fox, an opossum, owls and hawks—perch on the rafters, climb the walls, and sit on tables waiting stoically to be examined. Environmental education exhibits and displays help fill the room, and children will especially like a hands-on nature exhibit.

In another wing a wide variety of science and nature programs are regularly presented in a comfortable auditorium. Nature films feature National Geographic and Disney releases, and a lecture se-

ries covers nature topics from around the globe, such as hikers who visited the Galapagos Islands and a naturalist's tour of Shenandoah National Park. Close-to-home nature study isn't overlooked, and sometimes the lectures move into a more natural setting outside.

County/City: Macomb/Sterling Heights

Fees: None.

Schedule: Monday-Thursday, 1-5 p.m.; Friday, closed; Saturday, 10 a.m.-5 p.m.; Sunday 1-5 p.m.

Directions: From M-59 about one mile west of M-53, turn south onto Van Dyke Rd. and go about one mile to Utica Rd. Turn left (east) onto Utica and drive one block to the nature center.

Further Information: Sterling Heights Nature Center, 42700 Utica Rd., Sterling Heights, MI 48078; (313) 739-6731.

122 BELLE ISLE

Belle Isle—at 985 acres, America's largest island urban park—had rather humble origins. Purchased from the Indians for three rolls of tobacco, eight barrels of rum, six pounds of red paint and one belt of wampum, the island was used by early Detroit settlers as a giant pigpen, where porkers could roam free yet remain relatively safe from wolves. It was still known as Hog Island when families first began sailing to it in the mid-1800s for picnics.

Today the only pigs on the island are those being barbecued. Around the turn of the century, well known landscape architect Frederick Law Omstead, who also created New York's Central Park, fashioned Belle Isle into an urban playground that is so big, with so much to see and do, that you have to come several times to take it all in.

What's immediately evident on your first visit is the unique and unavoidable scenery. Belle Isle is shaped like a giant ore carrier, and it sits in the middle of the Detroit River with its "prow" pointed downstream and tethered to the mainland by the MacArthur Bridge. A multilane one-way road circles the "deck" of this grounded ship, and from the 10-mile route, you're treated to some of the most striking scenery in southeast Michigan. Motorists, as well as joggers and bicyclists, move past quiet lagoons, deep woods, sprawling picnic areas, and Scott Fountain, which stands 38 feet tall and has 109 water outlets. The skylines of Windsor and Detroit make great backgrounds for watching pleasure craft and ore carriers that ply the river. The park also seems to extend an open invitation to walk along the edge of the river or slip down the quiet byways that cut through the heart of the island.

Thousands of visitors come daily to enjoy a meal in the park's almost unlimited picnic areas. The huge grounds can accommodate the largest party or family reunion, yet couples and small families can find a spot that offers scenery, seclusion or shade, and sometimes all three. Tables

edge the deep woods on the island's east end, they line the riverbank and frame the half-mile-long swimming beach on the north side, and they are scattered over picturesque meadows throughout the rest of the park.

The island is also one of the best birdwatching areas in the state. The park's lagoons and lakes attract numerous ducks in the fall. Many waterfowl winter-over on the Detroit River, and spring brings loons, grebes, warblers, woodpeckers, countless sparrows, and renewed flights of ducks.

Ball diamonds, basketball courts, tennis courts, a 20-station physical fitness trail, a golf course, and a huge play area with a giant amusement-park slide are among facilities that elevate the park well above the normal.

And there's more. An array of special attractions makes Belle Isle unique in the Midwest, if not the country.

(continued on p. 124)

Southeastern Lower Peninsula

(continued from p. 123)

NATURE CENTER

The entire park will delight nature lovers, but they will be especially drawn to the Nature Center, on the northeast end of the island. There, two narrow self-guided footpaths lead away from the island's hustle and bustle into nearly 200 acres of virgin timber and around wetlands filled with wildlife. Visually handicapped visitors can also experience nature on a sensory trail near the center. Inside the modern building, exhibits and displays showcase Michigan plants and animals, and park naturalists conduct weekend programs. You can walk the trails any time, but the building is only open noon to 4 p.m. on Tuesdays and 10 a.m. to 4 p.m. Wednesday through Sunday.

BELLE ISLE ZOO

East Indian apes, South American bears, kangaroos, sea lions, wolves, big cats and exotic birds are just a few of the fascinating animals you can see wandering their large, barless, natural confines at this 13-acre zoo, located near the center of the island. You get unobstructed close-up views from an elevated boardwalk that winds through the enclosures, and a trip to the zoo can be the high point of a child's visit to Belle Isle. The zoo is open daily 10 a.m. to 5 p.m. from May through October. Admission is free for children under five and $2 for adults, with discounts for senior citizens and children between the ages of five and 12.

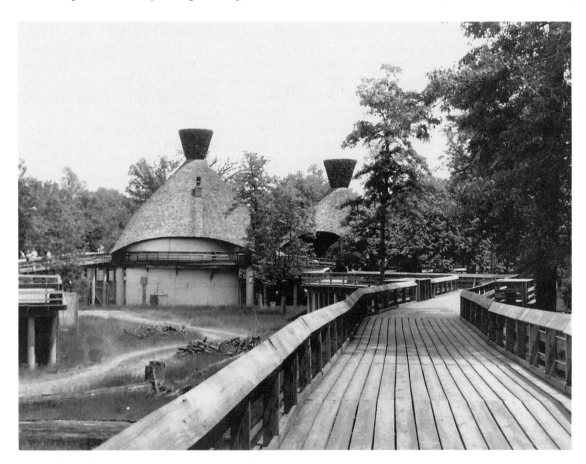

WHITCOMB CONSERVATORY

A quarter of a million plants inside, plus countless others in formal gardens surrounding Whitcomb Conservatory attract a million visitors a year. Inside the towering glass structure, six display rooms showcase tropical plants, ferns, cactus, palms, and special displays that erupt in wild splashes of color. The Tropical Room alone is worth a visit to examine breadfruit, pomegranate, papaya and coffee trees and take in the exquisite beauty of orchids, hibiscus and a variety of exotic plants. Outside, a lily pond, an outstanding display of perennials, and the formal gardens that surround the conservatory are also lovely. And in the spring, 40,000 tulips and 1,250 narcissi paint the landscape with a variety of vibrant colors. The conservatory hosts six major flower shows throughout the year. The building is open daily from 9 a.m. to dusk, and admission is free.

AQUARIUM

Unless you scuba dive, there's no better or easier way to see live fish in their natural element than beneath the sea-green tile of Belle Isle Aquarium's arched ceiling. More than 40 large tanks line the walls of this, the nation's oldest freshwater aquarium. Fish native to the Great Lakes region dominate the collection of 5,000 live specimens representing 118 species. But stingrays, Australian lungfish, and the gourami—a species that has been around for 26 million years and looks it—are just a few of the weird, colorful and remarkably ugly fish from around the world that draw more than their fair share of stares. The aquarium is open daily from 10 a.m. to 5 p.m., and admission is free.

DOSSIN GREAT LAKES MUSEUM

The romance and history of the Great Lakes lives on at the Dossin Great Lakes Museum. The lounge of a Great Lakes passenger ship, an authentic pilot house, artifacts from shipwrecks, a large collection of model ships, and a variety of other special exhibits trace the history of seafaring on the lakes. The museum is open 10 a.m. to 5:30 p.m. Wednesday through Saturday. Admission is free.

County/City: Wayne/Detroit

Fees: None.

Schedule: Open all year. For specific days and times, refer to the description of each attraction in the main text.

Directions: From the junction of I-375 and Jefferson Ave. in downtown Detroit, drive approximately 2.5 miles northeast on Jefferson to E. Grand River Blvd. Turn right and cross MacArthur Bridge to the park.

Southeastern Lower Peninsula

123 CRANBROOK INSTITUTE OF SCIENCE

Botany, zoology, mineralogy, geology, archeology, anthropology, physics, astronomy—Cranbrook Institute of Science introduces the entire spectrum of the physical sciences to the curious. Not curious? You will be before you finish touring what has been called one of America's most important natural history museums. It's hard not to look through the museum's telescope, watch a working beehive, view the skeleton replica of one of the earliest known humans, or study the remains of dinosaurs without coming away with a feeling of awe for the immense diversity of our world and its natural history. And like any great museum, Cranbrook not only stirs your curiosity, but also stimulates a long-lasting interest in and appreciation for our planet.

Though the museum is well organized into collections representing the fundamental disciplines of the physical and life sciences, it's impossible to take in everything in a single visit. Just the collection of beautiful, diverse, and, yes, delicate minerals and crystals, for instance, numbers more than 2,500 specimens, making it the eighth-largest in North America. And you can spend hours in the Physics Room manipulating 60 hands-on, do-it-yourself experiments that introduce light, sound, electricity, the laws of motion, and other principles of physical science.

Other major exhibit areas combine lifelike dioramas, displays and exhibits with some kind of hands-on or other participatory experience. In the anthropology hall, for instance, a display of American Indian artifacts is not far from a computer you can use to learn more about human evolution.

In another section of the museum, incredibly realistic dioramas not only re-create Michigan's various biosystems, but also suspend a bit of nature drama in time. When you walk up to one of the many picture windows, you get the feeling that, as if by magic, you have walked into a hardwood forest in southern Michigan, or paused in a sunny tall-grass meadow, or hiked into the dunes along Lake Michigan, or become lost in a coniferous forest in the Upper Peninsula. And when you look carefully, you'll see animals native to each ecosystem freeze-framed in the act of living out their lives amid the beautifully preserved wildflowers, shrubs, grasses and trees.

On Saturday nights you can also look to the heavens through a six-inch refracting telescope, which is housed at one end of the museum in Michigan's only public observatory. Or, at the opposite end of the building, you can get a simulated look at the cosmos at the state's busiest planetarium, with scheduled shows on weekends throughout the year and daily during July and August and on holidays.

While the museum illustrates the natural history of the whole world, an adjacent nature center lets you experience a small part of it. A working beehive and a large collection of stuffed birds and animals are among exhibits that fill an interpretive building. A large picture window overlooks an outdoor bird feeding area, and a three-quarter-mile self-guided trail leads from the center through a quiet corner of the sprawling Cranbrook complex. Most of the grounds are beautifully and expertly landscaped, but the nature trail winds through woods, a swamp and open fields designed only by nature.

County/City: Oakland/Bloomfield Hills

Fees: Adults, $3; Senior citizens and students (5-17), $2.

Schedule: Mon. through Fri., 10 a.m.-5 p.m.; Fri. night, 7 p.m.-10 p.m.; Sat., 10 a.m.-10 p.m.; and Sun., 1-5 p.m. The nature center is open on Saturday and Sunday from 1 p.m. to 5 p.m. during the winter, and daily 1 p.m. to 5 p.m. in the summer.

Directions: Cranbrook Institute is located on Lone Pine Rd. between Woodward and Telegraph in the city of Bloomfield Hills.

Further Information: Cranbrook Institute of Science, 500 Lone Pine Rd., P.O. Box 801, Bloomfield Hills, MI 48013; (313) 645-3200.

124 CRANBROOK GARDENS

The view of the grounds from the west terrace of the Cranbrook Estate leaves no room for doubt that you are overlooking one of the great formal gardens in the Midwest.

George Booth and his wife, Ellen Scripts Booth, built a huge English country manor on rolling Oakland County farmland in 1908. In keeping with the beautiful mansion, they designed and built a formal gardens on the west side of the house. In 1934 the Booths donated the gardens to Cranbrook Institute, which not only maintained their original beauty, but also made them available for all of us to enjoy.

Within the 12-foot-high fieldstone walls that frame the garden area, 5,000 annuals fill your eyes with a kaleidoscope of color and beauty, which reaches its peak of magnificence in late summer. Red brick walkways, gravel paths, sculptures, fountains and pools add to the enchantment of the scene, and because different flowers are planted each year, the show changes from summer to summer.

Dazzling landscaping isn't confined to the formal garden. At the back of the house, a spacious lawn sweeps down to a manmade lake, and you can find countless specimen trees throughout the grounds. An oriental garden, a Greek theater, a natural-looking grove of pine trees, a field sprinkled every spring with over a thousand daffodils, a rock garden, redbud and dogwood trees, massed plantings of perennials, and ornamental shrubs all ensure an ever-changing show from spring to fall.

County/City: Oakland/Bloomfield Hills

Fees: Adults—$2; Senior citizens, students, children—$1.50.

Schedule: June, July, August—Mon. through Sat., 10 a.m.-5 p.m.; Sunday, 1-5 p.m. May and September—Mon. through Sat., 1-5 p.m.; Sunday, 1-5 p.m. October—Weekends only, 1-5 p.m.

Directions: The gardens are located at 380 Lone Pine Rd., between Telegraph (US-24) and Woodward Ave. (US-10). Park either on Lone Pine Rd. across from the entrance or in the Christ Church Cranbrook parking lot.

Further Information: Cranbrook House and Gardens, 380 Lone Pine Rd., Box 801, Bloomfield Hills, MI 48303; (313) 645-3149.

125 JOHNSON NATURE CENTER

Surrounded by expressways and the hustle and bustle of a busy suburban community, the E.J. Johnson Nature Center gives refuge to fox, pheasants, a woodchuck, raccoons, squirrels, two penned deer, a pair of caged Red-tail Hawks, and people seeking temporary escape from city life.

Owned and operated by the Bloomfield Hills School District, the 32-acre center is a "special outdoor learning area set aside to develop and encourage outdoor/environmental/ ecological education and activities for students and community." To that end the nature center's educational programs are an integral part of the school district's curriculum from kindergarten through high school. Year-round programming for adults includes ecology walks, bird-banding demonstrations, and maple sugar making.

Or you can skip the formal programs and just take a quiet, peaceful walk along any of five nature trails that wind through the preserve's acreage, which is almost equally divided between woodland and open fields. Six miles of trails cut through an impressive stand of pine, border a large tree-lined pond, pass a maple sugar shack, and edge pleasant meadows. A small stream, native wildflowers, and the rocky debris from glaciers that passed this way thousands of years ago add interest to any walk. Many of the trees and shrubs along the routes are labeled and one of the trails is self-guided, so even an informal outing can turn into an educational experience.

The wide diversity of habitat, good cover and several feeding stations encourage numerous birds to set up housekeeping here, so bring binoculars and a bird identification book.

Children will be especially delighted with two penned deer that are so tame they walk up to the fence and almost ask to be petted.

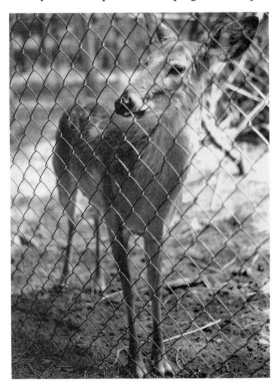

County/City: Oakland/Bloomfield Hills

Fees: None.

Schedule: School Year—Open to the public from 10 a.m. to 4 p.m. on Saturday and Sunday of the second weekend of each month.
Summer—Weekdays, 8 a.m. to 5 p.m.; Weekend schedule is the same as during the school year.

Directions: From Pontiac, drive about 2 miles south on M-24 to Lone Pine Rd. Turn right (west) onto Lone Pine and go one block to Franklin Rd. Turn right (north) onto Franklin and drive 1/2 mile to the entrance.

Further Information: E.J. Johnson Nature Center, 3325 Franklin Rd., Bloomfield Hills, MI 48013.

126 ADDISON OAKS COUNTY PARK

Don't think of this 700-acre outdoor playground as just a county park, but rather as a full-service resort. Whether for a day trip or a week-long camping vacation, there's something at Addison Oaks—with its spring-fed lakes, hiking and biking trails, campgrounds, and much more—to keep just about everyone busy. Or if busy doesn't fit into your definition of a vacation, there's also plenty of opportunity for solitude and do-nothing relaxation amid striking natural beauty.

Near the park entrance, an immense picnic area spreads over a lush lawn the envy of most home owners. You can pick from both sunny and shady sites, and many of the tables and grills cozy up to two spring-fed lakes that flank the area. Other facilities at the huge outdoor dining area include pavilions and a large playground.

The crystal-clear waters of Bruhl Lake make an inviting swimming hole, especially from a sandy area that fronts the east side of the picnic grounds. There's no public launch onto Bruhl and the park's other lake, pond-size Lake Adam, but fishermen and boaters can coast across their quiet waters in rental rowboats and pedal boats.

Etching the park's eastern half are four hiking trails, totaling over four miles in length, that follow the shore of Bruhl lake, cross open meadows, pass small wetlands, and roll over countryside studded with stands of pine, sugar maple, willow and oak.

For some real exercise, bring your mountain bike and cruise four miles of mountain bike trails that furrow the western half of the park. Four main trails and their connecting loops make it possible for pedalers to complete a circuit of less than a mile or bull their way through the full four-mile-route through the rolling countryside.

Near the back of the park, two pretty campgrounds snuggle in the woods away from most of the day-use activities. At a modern campground in a small meadow surrounded by woods, 50 spacious, grass-carpeted sites with concrete slips and electric and water hookups are all close to a modern restroom building. A rustic 50-site campground is laid out in deep shade next to the largest tract of undisturbed woodland in the park.

Fun doesn't stop when the snow falls. Thirteen miles of groomed snowmobile trails snake through the park, and skaters and fisherman dot the two lakes when they freeze over. A popular sledding hill lures kids and families.

A bountiful variety of Michigan flora grows in the park, and future development plans include a 15-acre botanical garden and arboretum.

Birdwatching opportunities are excellent.

County/City: Oakland/Rochester

Fees: A daily vehicle permit is $2.50 for residents and $4.50 for non-residents.

Schedule: Memorial Day to Labor Day, 8 a.m.-10 p.m.; Fall and Spring, 8 a.m.-10 p.m. weekends only; Snowmobile Season, 10 a.m.-10 p.m. weekends only.

Directions: From Rochester drive approximately 8 miles north on Rochester Rd. to Romeo Rd. Turn left (west) onto Romeo and drive 2 miles to the park entrance.

Further Information: Addison Oaks County Park, 1480 W. Romeo Rd., Oxford, MI 48051; (313) 693-2432.

Southeastern Lower Peninsula

127 ORION OAKS COUNTY PARK

Most people will look at this 927-acre tract of Oakland County land and think about what a nice park it will be, once developed. Nature lovers will see a lush, wild tract of land that suits them just fine as is.

The park's master plan, expected to be implemented over the next few years, includes camping, boating, picnic and fishing facilities, plus a nature study area. But what you get until then is a land of open meadows, stands of dense woods, wetlands, and—a true rarity for Oakland County—a 90-acre lake totally devoid of development.

There are no marked trails, but there is plenty of room to wander wherever you like. From the entrance on Joslyn Road, you can pick your way along the edge of quiet Lake Sixteen. Broad wetlands border much of the lake's irregular shoreline, and numerous ducks, geese, swans, herons and other shorebirds find refuge in the narrow inlets and marshy edges. If you come equipped with a spotting scope or binoculars, even the parking lot is a good vantage point for picking out waterfowl during spring migration.

For more-wide-open spaces and good chances for spotting even more birds, squeeze through a gap in the fence at the park's service entrance, a half mile west of Joslyn Road on Clarkston Road. After a short walk south, you'll reach a high, open meadow ringed by distant woods and dotted with shrubby vegetation. No trails crease the fields, but you're free to look where you want for woodland birds and species that favor open spaces.

County/City: Oakland/Clarkston

Fees: None.

Schedule: None posted.

Directions: From I-75 take the Joslyn Rd. exit (#83) and go approximately 3 miles north on Joslyn Rd.

This five-acre pie-shaped piece of land, squeezed between a marshy stream and a section of Grand Trunk Railroad tracks, shelters a precious slice of Michigan real estate. Except for the possibility of some gravel removal from a small hill, this Michigan Nature Association-owned parcel is a piece of the less than one quarter of one percent of Oakland County's original land cover that remains untouched by humans.

It's a living biological museum that shows what this section of our state looked like before it was drained, plowed, leveled and subdivided. Packed within the little triangle of land, you'll find both a wet and a dry prairie, a small creek narrow enough to step across, a fen, a bog, a marsh, and a gravel ridge that runs down its middle parallel to the railroad tracks.

From a short trail that creases the top of the gravelly ridge, you get some good views east, where the land slips down to the picturesque creek, which winds through a marshy wetlands. Tamaracks edge the far side of the fast-moving stream, and rising hills blanketed in hardwoods frame the scene.

The preserve's importance as a refuge for Michigan flora surpasses its scenic beauty. The striking diversity of landscape nurtures an amazing 289 different species of native Michigan plants, some of which bear equally amazing names such as golden alexanders, bastard toadflax, pussy toes, cotton grass, New Jersey tea and hoary puccoon. From mid-May through mid-September, eye-catching wildflowers are everywhere underfoot. You don't have to carry a wildflower identification guide to enjoy a visit, but it does add to richness of the experience.

Bluebird boxes dot the preserve, and the marsh, creek, and surrounding wooded area present fair opportunities for birdwatching.

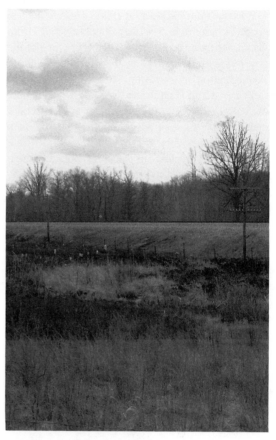

County/City: Oakland/Holly

Fees: None.

Schedule: Open all year.

Directions: From Holly, drive 2 miles south on Milford Rd. about 2 miles to Rattalee Rd. Turn left (east) onto Rattalee and drive approximately 2 miles to the preserve, on the south side of the road. Or from Clarkston, drive north on Dixie Hwy. approximately 5 miles to Rattalee Rd. Turn left (west) onto Rattalee and drive approximately 4 miles to the preserve.

Further Information: Michigan Nature Association, 7981 Beard Rd., Box 102, Avoca, MI 48006.

Howell Nature Center operates one of the few hospitals where well-wishers benefit more from visitations than the patients. The center, one of the few Michigan members of the National Wildlife Rehabilitation Association, takes in orphaned, sick, injured and confiscated wildlife with the goal of returning them to the wild. The animals could care less about human visitors, and the hours open to the public are very limited. But it's well worth a trip here to get close-up views of both common and exotic animals and gain a renewed appreciation for the diversity and beauty of the animal kingdom.

Approximately 100 birds and mammals are in treatment at any one time, and the 40-plus pens and cages that hold them line a short trail that circles a pond near the headquarters. A recent patient list included a Turkey Vulture, a Red-tail Hawk, a coyote, an Arctic fox, raccoons, squirrels, a Great Horned Owl, deer, a Great Blue Heron, doves, songbirds, a pheasant, a Kestrel, rabbits, a ferret and a family of ducks. You can never be sure what you might see, because each year the center receives over 500 birds and animals representing approximately 50 different species. Labels at most cages identify each animal and sometimes describe its natural habitat and range.

There's more on Howell Nature Center's 260 gently rolling acres than just an animal hospital. Five miles of hiking and cross country ski trails, which vary from one half to four miles in length, cut through a mature hardwood forest and cross open fields studded with wildflowers. Cross country ski rentals are available.

In December the center hosts a choose-and-cut Christmas tree sale from their tree nursery.

The main emphasis at Howell Nature Center, which is owned by the Presbytery of Detroit, is outdoor and environmental education. The center's year-round staff conducts over 75 different programs for student groups who visit the 260-acre outdoor classroom. The programs can be tailored to students from kindergarten through high school and vary in length from an hour to a several-day stay at the center's lodge.

County/City: Livingston/Howell

Fees: Classes pay a minimal fee per student. Visits to the animal hospital and use of trails is free.

Schedule: The center hosts an open house for the general public nearly every Sunday from 1-4 p.m., but call ahead.

Directions: From I-96 on the south side of Howell, take exit 137 and drive south on Pinckney Rd. approximately 4.5 miles to Triangle Lake Rd. Turn right (west) onto Triangle and drive one mile to the nature center.

Further Information: Howell Nature Center, 1005 Triangle Lake Rd., Howell, MI 48843; (517) 546-0249.

130 PARK LYNDON

Unlike most county parks, Park Lyndon was not designed to cater to hordes of summer picnickers, partiers and water enthusiasts. You won't find any ball diamonds, swimming beaches, or large picnic or play areas. What you will find is 205 beautiful acres of gently rolling, but often steep, hilly terrain that not only contains nearly every type of habitat known to southern Michigan, but also has been nearly undisturbed by man since the passing of the glaciers.

When the glaciers let go of Michigan some 10,000 years ago, they left a rich and varied landscape that Europeans, almost from their first settling, did everything to change. They mined, lumbered, plowed, drained and leveled the land. But Park Lyndon was spared, and today you can witness the work of the glaciers at nearly every turn. Glacial lakes, swamps, bogs, and long, narrow ribbons of gravel called eskers, which were once streams within the mile-thick slabs of ice, create an ever-changing landscape.

The park is a naturalist's playground, and with binoculars, bird books, and tree and wildflower identification guides, you can spend a day lost in revery. You can even sample the edible nuts and berries that grow along the trails, but you can't collect them in bulk or remove them from the park.

North Territorial Road divides Park Lyndon into two distinct north/south sections. Much of the south parcel was used for grazing until the 1940s, but today you'll find little, if any, evidence of its pasture days. A thick, vine-draped oak/hickory forest covers the steep hillsides, and pine plantations, aging meadows and wetlands blanket other parts of the acreage.

Several trails, some up to four miles long, wander through the varying landscape of the park's south section. A few cut through woods so peaceful and quiet that the rustle of squirrels and chipmunks scurrying across the leaf-covered forest floor may startle you. The shortest trail falls sharply down to lily-pad-covered Lake Genevieve. The lake's shoreline is an indistinct marshy transition between water and terra firma, but two observation decks reach out from the shore to provide excellent views of the glassy-smooth water, which is populated by countless turtles, frogs, dragonflies and an occasional snake.

The main trail into the park's northern acreage, which has barely felt a touch from the hand of man, begins near the parking area on a high, open ridge but quickly plunges into a cool, shaded forest on a long descent that ends at a large expanse of marsh, swamp and wetlands named the Embury Swamp Natural Area. You can get glimpses of tuliptrees, tamaracks, and some of Michigan's rarest flora, including 23 species of ferns and 10 types of orchids, from the combination of corduroy paths, boardwalks and trails that traverse that natural area.

Two small picnic areas—each with tables, grills and a small pavilion—are located at the trailheads, one on each side of North Territorial Road.

County/City: Washtenaw/Chelsea

Fees: None.

Schedule: Open all year, 8 a.m. to dusk.

Directions: From US-23 5 miles north of Ann Arbor, exit onto North Territorial Rd. and drive west 18 miles. Or, from M-52 about 6 miles north of Chelsea, turn right (east) onto North Territorial and go one mile.

Further Information: Washtenaw County Parks, P.O. Box 8645, Ann Arbor, MI 48107.

Southeastern Lower Peninsula

131 INDEPENDENCE LAKE PARK

Independence Lake Park has all the makings for a good-old-fashioned, something-for-everyone, day-long family picnic. A sprawling picnic grounds, large pavilions, sandy beach, several playground areas, fishing, boating, hiking, volleyball courts, and horseshoe pits—they're all there, spread over 312 beautiful acres.

The park's huge picnic area lines Independence Lake for several hundred yards and reaches back an almost equal distance from the shoreline. You can choose a relatively secluded table, either nestled at the edge of the woods well back from the lake or next to the water. Or you can set up right in the middle of all the action, near the busy swimming beach. (Four large pavilions, which seat from 90 to 480 people, are available on a rental basis and must be reserved in advance.)

The sandy beach indents the meadow in a long, sweeping arc, and if you like to spread a blanket and be slow-roasted by the sun, there's plenty of room to baste yourself on an adjacent, treeless football-field-size grassy lawn.

The park property takes in more than half the shoreline of Independence Lake, and you don't have to get wet to enjoy the emerald-green water. You can launch your boat at a ramp south of the beach, or you can rent a boat or canoe by the hour at the swimming beach. If you like to fish but prefer doing it from a rock-solid base rather than a rocking boat, you can wet your line from a handicapper-accessible fishing pier.

Away from the lake, a mile-plus nature trail probes the park's undeveloped land. The trail ambles from the parking lot down a wide two-track; passes over a marshy pond on a long, elevated boardwalk; then crosses the park road and loops through a succession of old meadows, where shrubs and small trees are slowly filling in the open spaces. Also along that loop, the path edges a lily-pad-choked pond and leads to a tall observation platform that overlooks the surrounding marsh and broken meadows. Except for a few

stands of mature hardwoods, most of what passes for woods here is young trees with a dense understory of shrubs and saplings.

Birdlife is abundant along the route. Bluebird boxes line parts of the trail, and it's possible to see Woodcock, pheasants, Catbirds, Cardinals, swallows, geese and ducks, all in one 10-minute span.

County/City: Washtenaw/Whitmore Lake

Fees: County residents, $2.50 daily, $15.00 seasonal; Non-residents, $4 daily, $25 seasonal; Senior citizens, $1.25 daily.

Schedule: Open all year.

Directions: From US-23 north of Ann Arbor, exit onto Six Mile Rd. and follow clearly marked signs approximately 4 miles to the park.

Further Information: Washtenaw County Parks and Recreation Commission, P.O. Box 8645, Ann Arbor, MI 48107.

132 DEXTER-HURON METROPARK and
133 DELPHI METROPARK

These similar parks—two companions in the 13-member Huron-Clinton Metropark system—nestle within lazy meanders of the Huron River. Dexter-Huron's 122 acres cover the north bank of a large bend in the river, and four miles downstream 45-acre Delphi Metropark fills in a large horseshoe loop on the south side of the river.

At each park, picnic tables and grills edge the quietly flowing water. At Delphi, which hugs the Huron for almost half a mile, widely spaced hardwoods and tall evergreens provide good shade close to the river. The picnic grounds at Dexter-Huron is larger, but stands of mature hardwoods and evergreens effectively break up the densely shaded area into smaller, more-private sites.

No formal trails mark either park, but at Delphi you can walk the long stretch of shoreline while watching the river sweep past gentlemanly trees that half bow over the water. You can usually spot ducks and geese, and a rapids at about the park's midpoint adds a nice counterpoint to the otherwise quiet flow. Back from the water, large, open meadows provide an alternative to the shaded riverbank area.

At both parks you can fish from the riverbank, and children and the young at heart will enjoy swings and slides.

Huron River Drive, which connects Delphi and Dexter-Huron by land, is a favorite with bicyclers. Either park makes an excellent staging area for unloading bikes from car carriers and then setting out on the approximately nine-mile round trip on the the asphalt road, which borders the river.

The stretch of river between the parks is heavily used by canoeists, and a canoe livery at Delphi offers daily put-in, pick-up trips between the two points.

County/City: Washtenaw/Ann Arbor

Fees: $2 for a daily vehicle permit, $10 for an annual permit. Senior citizens pay $5 annually.

Schedule: Open all year.

Directions: From M-14 on the north side of Ann Arbor, exit onto Huron River Dr. and go north 3 miles to Delphi or 7.5 miles to Dexter-Huron.

Further Information: Huron-Clinton Metropolitan Authority, 13000 High Ridge Dr., Brighton, MI 48116-8001; 1-800-247-2757.

Southeastern Lower Peninsula

134 NICHOLS ARBORETUM

Even though the University of Michigan's Nichols Arboretum is hard to get to, it consistently draws 100,000 visitors annually. If you pay even a brief visit, you'll see why. This is one of the premier arboretums in the Midwest, if not the country. Not only does it contain one of the most complete tree and plant collections in North America, but it's also one of the most delightful and pleasant locations in the state to take a walk or hike. In fact, it's not hard to imagine that Nichols Arboretum spawned the phrase "communing with nature."

Begun in 1907 on 27 acres, Nichols has grown to 130 acres. Its formal and natural settings of mature specimen plants plus large areas of totally untamed vegetation sprawl across a diverse landscape of steep ravines, open prairie and rolling hills, all fronted by a half-mile run of the Huron River.

Among the multitude of fascinating and impressive trees within the arboretum are 54 varieties labeled with small numbered tags that match a list in a brochure available by writing the university's School of Natural Resources (address below, right). With the help of that booklet, you can seek out Amur corktrees, cedar of Lebanon, Japanese zelkova, Japanese umbrella pine, baldcypress, and castor aralia, plus 27 species native to Michigan. Most of the trees are fully mature, and many are flowering varieties that put on a stunning spring show.

In early summer another attraction is worth a special visit. A peony garden contains over 220 varieties in 27 beds, and in June the 700 plants burst into a spectacular array of color. Another brochure, also available from the School of Natural Resources, identifies all the plants, some of which date back to 1927.

Several trails not only wind through lush vegetation past the outstanding examples of flora collected from all over the world, but also cross a 10-acre meadow choked with prairie grasses, border the Huron River, cut through primeval forests, and skirt small, marshy wetlands.

The arboretum is well-known among local birdwatchers as an excellent area to spot a surprisingly wide assortment of species. Spring migration brings an exceptional number of warblers to the wooded landscape, and Red-tailed Hawks and Cooper's Hawks have been known to nest in the area. Although spring and fall offer the best birding, a trip to the sanctuary any time of the year can be rewarding.

County/City: Washtenaw/Ann Arbor

Fees: None.

Schedule: Open all year, sunrise to sunset.

Directions: From the intersection of Washtenaw Ave. and Geddes Rd., on the east side of the central campus of the University of Michigan, drive east on Geddes about 2 blocks to Observatory St. Turn left (north) onto Observatory and go about 5 blocks to Washington Hts. Turn right (east) onto Washington and go to the arboretum entrance, at the end of the street just past the Ronald McDonald House.

Parking is a problem. On weekends, you may park in Hospital Lot M-29, which you can reach by driving on Observatory north a block past Washington Hts. to East Medical Campus Dr. and turning right. During the week, parking may or may not be available at the end of Washington Hts.

Further Information: Friends of Nichols Arboretum, University of Michigan, School of Natural Resources, Dana Bldg. 430 E. University, Ann Arbor, MI 48109.

135 ROLLING HILLS COUNTY PARK

Carved out of the rolling farmland of southeastern Washtenaw County, this new park has enough facilities and attractions to keep outdoor enthusiasts busy year round.

Near the center of the park, a pleasant picnic area snuggles in among a grove of young hardwoods that line one side of an oblong pond. Tables and grills are scattered among the thick-set trees, and from almost every picnic site you get good views of the pond and the rolling land across the narrow body of water. The pond also serves as a swimming hole, complete with a bathhouse and concession complex that are only a short walk from the picnic grounds.

An approximately half-mile-long nature trail, which circles around and over a wooded hill behind the picnic area, connects to a hiking/cross country ski trail. That three-mile-plus route crosses old farm fields, skirts large meadows, circles the pond, and ducks in and out of small woodlots as it traces the park's periphery.

The area is worth exploring by birders. Ducks visit the pond in spring, and the brushy fringe bordering the open fields plus the small, wooded groves should attract a fair share of songbirds.

A large water slide and pool will have kids clamoring to visit, and the outdoor fun doesn't stop when the snow flies. Three miles of cross country ski trails lace the park, and one loop is lighted for night skiing. A skating rink and toboggan run are added attractions, and you can rent ski equipment and toboggans.

County/City: Washtenaw/Ann Arbor

Fees: County residents, $2.50 daily vehicle permit, $15 annual; Non-residents, $4 daily, $25 annual; Senior citizens $1.25 daily.

Schedule: Open all year—Weekdays, 2-9 p.m.; Weekends and Christmas vacation, 10 a.m.-9 p.m..

Directions: From US-23 approximately 5 miles south of Ann Arbor, exit onto Willis Rd. and drive east 2 miles to Stoney Creek Rd. Turn left (north) onto Stoney Creek Rd. and drive 1.5 miles to the park entrance.

Southeastern Lower Peninsula

A fully restored, operating grist mill, which ground area farmers' feed from 1873 until 1968, is the focal point for most visitors at this Washtenaw County park. But nature lovers, birdwatchers, and anyone else who takes pleasure in a stroll through a quiet, pastoral landscape will find much more.

Fleming Creek, which powered the mill, is itself worth a visit. Almost small enough to jump, the exuberant little creek rushes over midstream boulders and recklessly weaves through curves. Mature, staid hardwoods that hover overhead seem to gaze disapprovingly at the stream's constant youthful frivolity. A short trail drops under a bridge that spans Geddes Road, then edges the stream as it tumbles over a short rapids. But if you want to follow the brook through most of the rest of the park, you have to carefully pick your way around and over streamside trees, roots and brush.

Developed trails do step into other areas of the 27-acre park, including a large meadow slowly being reclaimed by shrubs and young trees. The wide, easily walked trails pass through some excellent bird habitat—from dense thickets and open fields to the tree-lined creek—and birders should have good luck filling their binoculars from a variety of choice spots.

Adjacent to the parking lot, a small picnic area, consisting of just a few tables and no other facilities, overlooks both the mill and Geddes Road.

County/City: Washtenaw/Ann Arbor

Fees: None.

Schedule: The trails are open all year.

Directions: From US-23 on the east side of Ann Arbor, exit onto Geddes Rd. (exit 39) and drive east approximately one mile to the park entrance.

Further Information: Washtenaw County Parks and Recreation Commission, P.O. Box 8645, Ann Arbor, MI 48107-8645.

137   COUNTY FARM PARK

If you're tired of exercising in the artificial environment of a gym or health club, County Farm Park's outdoor fitness trails, which combine cardiovascular exercise stops with the enjoyment of nature, may be just what the waistline ordered. Or, the gravel paths through the varied and pretty scenery are enjoyable places to simply take a walk.

Three level, wide trails—which loop 0.6, 1.1 and 1.4 miles through the park—skirt deep woods, pass by a perennial demonstration garden and native shrub plantings, and cross meadows where shrubs and brush are filling the open spaces. At numerous stops along the routes, you can perform a variety of exercises on specially constructed equipment. Also, a 0.4-mile nature trail, with no fitness stops, weaves through a dense hardwood forest with a tangled understory of brush, saplings and wildflowers.

The shrub-filled meadows and wild, overgrown forest, all located within a densely populated urban area, make County Farm a small oasis for wildlife and also a prime birding spot.

A picnic area—tables, grills, and a small pavilion—at the Manchester Street entrance is too small to accommodate large groups, but for a family picnic, it's a nice alternative to busy parks or long drives.

In the winter a 1.5-mile cross country ski trail here is another option for exercising in the out-of-doors.

County/City: Washtenaw/Ann Arbor

Fees: None.

Schedule: Open all year, 8 a.m.-9 p.m.

Directions: Fitness and nature trailheads and the picnic pavilion are all at the park's east entrance. To get there, from the intersection of Manchester and Washtenaw (just east of the Stadium Blvd./Washtenaw Ave. junction, on the southeast side of Ann Arbor) go south on Manchester about 3 blocks to Medford. Turn left onto Medford and go less than 1/4 mile to the parking lot.

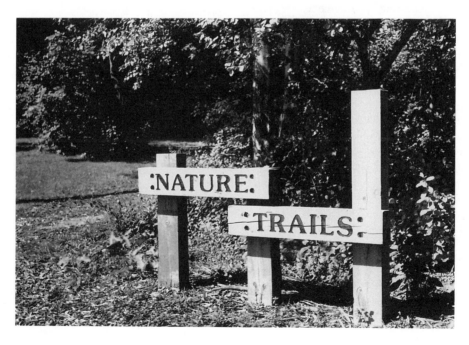

Southeastern Lower Peninsula

138 LOWER HURON METROPARK

This long, relatively narrow, 1,239-acre Huron-Clinton Metropark borders both banks of the Huron River for more than five miles. The river is the thread that binds this beautiful park together, because whether you are picnicking, hiking bird-watching, biking, or just enjoying a scenic drive, the wide, lazy stream is rarely out of view.

An access road runs through the park, and wide loops of the river continuously curve away from, then back to the edge of the pavement. At about the halfway point, the road crosses over the wide ribbon of water, then the river plays the same game on the opposite side. Strung along the road, nestled in the river's broad loops are picnic areas and playgrounds, a par-3 golf course, hiking trails, nature areas, ball fields, and a large swimming pool.

Bicyclists, joggers and walkers can take in five-plus miles of the beautiful scenery along a wide bike path that parallels the park road.

Hikers and nature lovers can choose from two trails through contrasting environments. A self-guiding brochure for both is available at the park office, and both offer good birding. The Bob White Nature Trail's woodchip-covered path winds for almost a mile through an upland hardwood forest on the side of the road opposite the river. The pleasant walk is especially rewarding in spring when wildflowers blanket the forest floor.

The Paw Paw Nature Trail drops to the flood plain of the Huron River, where the path then weaves through a lowland swamp marked by huge trees—many labeled—and a wild profusion of native Michigan flowers.

The park's picnic areas are the equal of any in southeastern Michigan for beauty and spaciousness. The tables, grills and shelters dot nearly endless expanses of lush grass, and most spots have the river as a backdrop and are shaded by stately trees.

During the winter you can skate on three lighted ponds or cross country ski anywhere other than the golf course.

County/City: Wayne/New Boston

Fees: Daily vehicle permit, $2; Annual vehicle permit, $10; Senior citizen annual permit, $5.

Schedule: Open year round, 6 a.m.-10 p.m.

Directions: From the junction of I-94 and I-275, drive south on I-275 4 miles to the Sibley Rd. exit. Go west 1/2 mile on Sibley to Huron River Dr. Turn left (south) onto Sibley and drive 1/2 mile to the park entrance.

Further Information: Lower Huron Metropark, 17845 Savage Rd., Belleville, MI 48111.

139 LOST NATION STATE GAME AREA

Even the area's oldest residents argue over the origin of the mysterious, rather romantic name of this wild and rugged section of Hillsdale County. Speculation has swung between the practical—it was "a good place to get lost in"—to wild fantasies, perhaps kindled by the prehistoric Indian mounds that dot the area, that it once harbored a lost tribe of mankind. Another theory has it that "lost nation" refers to the last remnant of Pottawatomi Indians that lived here before the government removed them to the west.

No matter how it got its name, the 2,374-acre checkerboard tract of land, which on a map looks like a flight of stairs climbing to the city of Hillsdale, is a wild and beautiful natural retreat in the heart of rich farming country. The heavily wooded terrain is crisscrossed by glacial ridges and pierced by the swift-flowing St. Joseph of the Maume River. The landscape constantly changes as you travel even short distances on the narrow dirt roads that subdivide the area. Occasional stretches of very rugged terrain alternate with low hills covered with mature stands of hardwoods, small lakes, swamps, and bright, little streams. In the 1850s Silas Doty, a notorious outlaw and self-proclaimed Robin Hood, used the area as a hideout, and it's easy to see why. On either foot or by car, you can become momentarily disoriented by the dense thickets and small pockets of wilderness that seem more appropriate to northern Michigan.

Raccoon, fox, pheasant and opossum roam the area, and birdwatching is good throughout. Wild Turkeys have recently been released here, and you could have your day made by catching a glimpse of one. Two endangered species—a small, white lady's slipper and Kirtland's water snake—have

(continued on p. 142)

Southeastern Lower Peninsula

LOST NATION STATE GAME AREA

(continued from p. 141)

been recorded in the area.

You can easily enjoy the scenery from a slow-moving car on the narrow dirt roads that grid the state game area. The lush vegetation, moving water, and occasional decaying structures that date back to the earliest settlers are among the ever-changing sights.

But the best way to appreciate and enjoy Lost Nation is on foot. There are no officially marked trails, but the combination of old roads now closed to motor traffic and many well-worn footpaths provide plenty of hiking opportunities. The state game area lies within a *V* formed by highways M-99 and M-34, and nearly all roads within the *V* that cross state land are dotted by parking areas from which you can head into the woods.

Jeff Greene from District 13 of the DNR, which administers Lost Nation, recommends several good areas for hikers. The nicest and easiest walking is on Way Road. To reach it drive about 3.5 miles east of the intersection of M-99 and M-34 on M-34 to Rumsey Road. Turn south onto Rumsey and go one mile to Way Road. Turn west onto Way and drive 0.4 mile to a small pulloff on the north side of the road where a barricaded gully and two-track come in from the north. Greene says the trail from there "follows a high ridge with mature oaks and hickories and ends when following the lefthand fork in the trail at the St. Joe of the Maume River."

You can reach another especially pretty site by driving farther west on Way Road until it ends at Tripp Road. Turn north onto Tripp and drive almost a mile to where a narrow dirt road intersects from the west. Within a few hundred yards of that intersection are four parking areas from which several unmarked trails lead into the forested hills.

Just east of Tripp Road, almost opposite the intersection, are the ruins of what looks like an old mill. You can see the stonework of the millrace, and the foundation of the mill itself rises a few feet above the ground. It is a delightful spot to pull off the road, enjoy the view of the river, eat a picnic lunch, and wonder about who, why and how

someone long ago started a business in this remote place.

Other suggested hikes by Greene begin at a parking area on Gilbert Road just south of Skuse Road and on and old two-track on Bowditch Trail a half mile east of Bird Lake Road.

Hikers may have even more choices in the near future, because the state game area is on the proposed route of the North Country Trail, which when completed will completely traverse both of Michigan's peninsulas.

County/City: Hillsdale/Hillsdale

Fees: None.

Schedule: Open all year, no posted schedule.

Directions: From the intersection of M-99 and M-34, you can access the area by driving east on M-34 and turning south onto either Bird Lake Rd., Tripp Rd., Rumsey Rd. or Pittsford Rd.

Further Information: Dept. of Natural Resources District 13, 3335 Lansing Ave., Jackson, MI 49202.

140 EMERY PARK

This unusual 90-acre picnic area is more water than land. Most of the park property, formerly the site of a fish hatchery, consists of large ponds bordered by tree-shaded lawns and circled by narrow gravel roads. In some cases the roads are the only thing separating the large pools.

Fishermen can lower hooks, lines and sinkers from short piers that jut out into the ponds. If the piers, which can comfortably hold only a couple of people, are filled, the grass-covered banks make just as convenient a fishing spot.

Solitary picnic tables dot the edges of the ponds, and some are close enough to the water to fish from. If you're nervous about mixing small children and water, you can picnic back from the ponds at more-secluded tables canopied by mature hardwoods. The park contains a pavilion and playground equipment.

Hiking here consists of wandering around the ponds on the park roads or strolling a short trail that weaves through trees bordering the park.

County/City: Hillsdale/Hillsdale

Fees: None.

Schedule: Open all year dawn to dusk.

Directions: From M-99 on the north side of Hillsdale, turn east onto Fayette St. and drive about one mile to where it deadends at Oak St. Turn right (south) onto Oak and go 3 blocks to State St. Turn left (east) onto State and drive 2 miles to the park.

Southeastern Lower Peninsula

141 SLAYTON ARBORETUM

Slayton Arboretum, on the campus of Hillsdale College, proves that an arboretum can have value far in excess of its scientific and educational purposes. The 72 acres of natural plantings, naturalistic landscaping and outstanding examples of fieldstone masonry is an aesthetic delight.

From a narrow, grass-covered plain enclosed by a fieldstone wall and marked by groupings of ornamental shrubs, mature trees and several ponds, the preserve climbs a hill blanketed by low-growing evergreens and tall pines, all accented by wildflowers. Most shrubs and trees bear identifying labels. A steep trail with large stone steps winds up the hill, which is also cut by a small manmade stream that ripples down the slope, tumbles over a waterfall, and comes to rest in a small, hidden pool. At the crest of the hill, a well-worn path follows the boundaries of the arboretum and offers good views of the grounds and plantings below.

Two fieldstone gazebos are the arboretum's two most distinctive manmade features. One overlooks the preserve from the top of the hill and, except for the profusion of trees and shrubs, may remind you of a German castle perched above the Rhine. The second gazebo is set beside a rock garden at the base of the hill within sight of a picturesque goldfish pond. A footbridge, amphitheater, fieldstone retaining walls, and two small fieldstone buildings add their charm to the surroundings.

You're welcome to wander anywhere along the grassy plain, and in addition to the main stone walkway, a series of other short trails wander up the hill and border its crest. The east edge of the arboretum ends at a wild, overgrown swamp pierced by a trail that can be wet and muddy in the spring.

The wide diversity of plant life, the good cover interspersed with open areas, and the marsh on the east attract a relatively large number of birds for such a small area, and the arboretum has long been a favored birdwatching site for area residents.

In addition to birds, the arboretum also draws brides and is a popular location for outdoor weddings. And when the snow flies, cross country skiers make tracks through the striking scenery.

County/City: Hillsdale/Hillsdale

Fees: None.

Schedule: Open dawn to dusk year round.

Directions: Located on the north side of the Hillsdale College campus, the arboretum is at the corner of Union and Barber streets, just north of the athletic field.

Further Information: Slayton Arboretum, Hillsdale College, Hillsdale, MI 49242.

ALPHABETICAL LISTING OF AREAS

(continued on p. 148)

ALPHABETICAL LISTING OF AREAS

(continued from p. 147)

BIRDWATCHING AREAS

AREAS WITH HIKING TRAILS

NATURE STUDY AREAS

AREAS WITH PICNIC SITES

🪑

ABRAMSON ROADSIDE PARK, p. 6
ADDISON OAKS COUNTY PARK, p. 129
ASPEN PARK, p. 58
BEAR RIVER VALLEY RECREATION
    AREA, p. 51
BELLE ISLE, p. 123
BERTRAND PARK, p. 94
BIG BEAR LAKE NATURE PATHWAY, p. 59
BROCK PARK, p. 101
BRUNO'S RUN HIKING TRAIL, p. 17
COOLEY BRIDGE, p. 79
CORSAIR TRAIL SYSTEM, p. 65
COUNTY FARM PARK, p. 139
COVERED BRIDGE COUNTY PARK, p. 98
CUT RIVER BRIDGE, p. 26
DELPHI METROPARK, p. 135
DEXTER-HURON METROPARK, p. 135
ELK RAPIDS COUNTY PARK, p. 71
EMERY PARK, p. 143
FOX PARK, p. 102
GORDON TURNER PARK, p. 35
HORSESHOE BAY WILDERNESS, p. 29
IMERMAN MEMORIAL PARK, p. 113
INDEPENDENCE LAKE PARK, p. 134
ISLAND LAKE RECREATION AREA, p. 66
JEWELL LAKE TRAIL, p. 60
KEWEENAW BAY SHORELINE DRIVE, p. 3
LAWLESS COUNTY PARK, p. 97
LODA LAKE WILDFLOWER SANCTUARY,
    p. 86

M-26, p. 2
MAGOON CREEK NATURAL AREA, p. 77
PAHL POINT PARK, p. 99
PARK LYNDON, p. 133
PARKER MILL, p. 138
PENINSULA POINT LIGHTHOUSE PARK,
    p. 19
PINES POINT RECREATION AREA, p. 85
POINT AUX CHENES, p. 28
PRESQUE ISLE COUNTY LIGHTHOUSE
    PARK, p. 36
PRESQUE ISLE LIGHTHOUSE, p. 38
PRESQUE ISLE PARK, p. 12
PRINISKI ROADSIDE PARK, p. 25
RINGWOOD FOREST, p. 116
RIVER ROAD NATIONAL FOREST SCENIC
    BYWAY, p. 61
ROLLING HILLS COUNTY PARK, p. 137
RUSS FOREST PARK, p. 96
SANFORD LAKE PARK, p. 111
SCOTT'S POINT, p. 24
SPORTSMEN'S PARK, p. 56
STATELINE NATIONAL RECREATION
    TRAIL, p. 7
VETERANS MEMORIAL PARK, p. 110
WAKELEY LAKE FOOT TRAVEL AREA,
    p. 68

SCENIC ATTRACTIONS

AREAS OF HISTORICAL INTEREST

AREAS WITH CROSS COUNTRY SKI TRAILS

ADDISON OAKS COUNTY PARK, p. 129
ANDERSON LAKE PATHWAY, p. 13
ASPEN PARK, p. 58
AVALANCHE PARK, p. 53
BEAR RIVER VALLEY RECREATION AREA, p. 51
BIG ISLAND LAKE WILDERNESS AREA, p. 23
BLACK RIVER PATHWAY, p. 10
CORSAIR TRAIL SYSTEM, p. 65
COUNTY FARM PARK, p. 139
DEERFIELD COUNTY PARK, p. 83
FOX PARK, p. 102
HOWELL NATURE CENTER, p. 132
IMERMAN MEMORIAL PARK, p. 113
JOHNSON NATURE PRESERVE, p. 41
LAWLESS COUNTY PARK, p. 97
LOST TAMARACK PATHWAY, p. 39
LOWER HURON METROPARK, p. 140

MCCORMICK WILDERNESS TRACT, p. 9
MCCUNE NATURE PRESERVE, p. 52
MT. MCSAUBA RECREATION AREA, p. 54
NORTH POINT PRESERVE, p. 54
PINE BOWL PATHWAY, p. 32
PINE HAVEN RECREATION AREA, p. 109
PRESQUE ISLE PARK, p. 12
RINGWOOD FOREST, p. 116
RIVER ROAD NATIONAL FOREST SCENIC BYWAY, p. 61
ROLLING HILLS COUNTY PARK, p. 137
SAND DUNES CROSS COUNTRY SKI TRAIL, p. 27
SHEEP RANCH PATHWAY, p. 80
SLAYTON ARBORETUM, p. 144
WAKELEY LAKE FOOT TRAVEL AREA, p. 68
WARNER CREEK PATHWAY, p. 57
WILDWOOD HILLS PATHWAY, p. 40

AREAS WITH SWIMMING BEACHES

ADDISON OAKS COUNTY PARK, p. 129
ANDERSON LAKE PATHWAY, p. 13
BEAVER ISLAND, p. 42
BELLE ISLE, p. 123
DEERFIELD COUNTY PARK, p. 83
FOX PARK, p. 102
INDEPENDENCE LAKE PARK, p. 134
ISLAND LAKE RECREATION AREA, p. 66

JEWELL LAKE TRAIL, p. 60
KEWEENAW BAY SHORELINE DRIVE, p. 3
PRESQUE ISLE COUNTY LIGHTHOUSE PARK, p. 36
PRESQUE ISLE PARK, p. 12
ROLLING HILLS COUNTY PARK, p. 137
SANFORD LAKE PARK, p. 111

CAMPING AREAS

SCENIC DRIVES

THE AUTHOR

Tom Powers is the Supervisor of Services to Adults and Outreach at the Flint Public Library. He has authored two previous books: *Natural Michigan: A Guide to 165 Michigan Natural Attractions* and *Michigan State and National Parks: A Complete Guide*.

When not at the library or researching and writing about the state he loves, Tom can usually be found dividing his time between reading, birdwatching, traveling and cooking.

Barbara, his wife of 27 years, and his two children and their spouses bring constant joy to his life.